The Red Coat

Surviving the Loneliness of Growing Up Within "The Secret Sect"

Peter Robertson

The Red Coat
Surviving the Loneliness of Growing Up Within "The Secret Sect"
by Peter Robertson

First published in Australia by Peter Robertson 2020
www.purplehousenaturaltherapies.com.au
For permissions: Peter Robertson
gro42768@gmail.com

A catalogue record for this
book is available from the
National Library of Australia

NATIONAL
LIBRARY
OF AUSTRALIA

ISBN: 978-0-6483820-3-4 (pbk)
ISBN: 978-0-6483820-4-1 (ebk)

Typesetting and design by Publicious Book Publishing
Published in collaboration with Publicious Book Publishing
www.publicious.com.au

Dedication

To Grada, who taught me to love and nurture myself, so that I may never again feel alone.

Also to Johanan, Lisanne, Caleb, Eve, Mieke and Tom my amazing children, who helped write the next chapter of my rewarding yet somewhat tumultuous life.

All One

Sitting on an isolated, lonely cliff face looking out over the sea, I thought of *Jonathan Livingston Seagull*. When I was in my teens he had resonated so deeply with my feelings of isolation and loneliness. Here it was once again, that feeling creeping back in with those desolate emotions of separateness. What had happened? How had I arrived here again? It seemed like history was cruelly repeating itself.

What was it trying to tell me?

Would I jump off this time and end my anguish?

Throughout my life I have felt misunderstood, not good enough, accused, despised even, until I dropped into a chasm of despair so deep it often took days to resurface.

Deep in my private desolation, I wondered if the lonely looking sky was trying to tell me something, when I noticed how effortlessly the clear azure sky blended with the sea - it was as if they were all one!

Perhaps for the first time I felt the true wonder of it. With each breath I became a part of the expanse of water, sky and time, no longer alone.

Alone … All One.

We are born part of the All One, but our reactions to life and all that we are taught often lead us to forget. Finally, I remembered, and understood how easily I could just become part of the 'All One' again.

As my mind and body eased, torment and regret replaced by an almost overwhelming sense of love and gratitude, my thoughts began wandering to the Red Coat.

Contents

· CHAPTER 1 ·

Body Blow

"Is that the best you could do, Ethel?"

That's not my first memory, but is likely amongst the first words I heard as a newborn, arriving home in my bassinet to be proudly displayed to my grandparents.

Grandma wasn't a very cheerful lady. I was born two weeks overdue, which she would have blamed me for, and my grandparents' holiday in Tasmania had come to an end. Thus, we met briefly at the door as they were rushing out, in a hurry to catch their plane home to mainland Australia.

I often wonder what Grandma's harsh words ringing in my little ears have sown in my life. Maybe nothing, as apparently I was a happy little chappy, at least according to my mum, who of course wouldn't have been biased one little bit.

One of my first memories, thankfully happier than meeting Grandma, was the simple exhilaration of catching my first fish. Mum and Dad were busy moving to a new house, from Roland to our new farm near Sprent (North West Tasmania), a step up for them. I was probably a nuisance, being only four years old, so was shepherded off to stay with friends who lived half an hour's drive away at Lower Barrington.

Sarah, the eldest daughter, must have had the job of keeping me happy, so she took me fishing at their dam. I felt a tug or two on my line, then Sarah helped me reel in a real little beauty, a trout. My first fish! How happy I felt, jumping up and down with joy. That memory remains etched in my brain. What had transpired prior to this, I can't remember, though I have heard stories bantered around the kitchen table of the first years of my life.

The seventh child in our large family, I was born in 1958, about three years after my twin brothers. My parents hadn't had an easy life at that point. They eked out a modest living milking cows on a small sixty-acre farm at Roland, where they'd moved after the birth of their eldest child, Joe, a son and heir to carry on the family name. A lot of the work in those days was done by horse, so Dad had bought a couple of capable workhorses, known for their quiet nature and being easy to handle. Mum was pregnant with my second eldest brother at that time, and Sunday afternoons were often whiled away with the young couple going for walks, proudly surveying their newly acquired real estate.

The story goes that on one such afternoon they were enjoying the sun on their backs as they ambled across a paddock, going slowly so Joe, who had just started walking, could keep up. He'd lagged behind, stumbling often with his newfound independence. Mum believed he was probably quietly picking daisies in the paddock, when suddenly one of the horses trotted over to him, turned, and lashed out with both back feet.

As Joe gazed innocently at the beauty around him, the horse's hooves connected with his fair little head.

My parents heard a plaintive cry, then nothing.

Racing to pick up their beautiful little boy, their hearts must have near stopped when they saw his head, misshapen by the blow of the hooves.

They sped to Sheffield Hospital, my mother nursing him in the front of the car and listening intently for signs of life, while Dad frantically drove. He was transferred immediately to Devonport Hospital, the closest major hospital. When my parents arrived, he was under observation and they could do nothing but watch and wait. His head was twice its normal size, swollen grotesquely, his eyes squeezed shut. Apparently, being so young, his cranial bones hadn't fused yet. This was lucky for him, my parents were told, as it meant the pressure wasn't squashing his brain.

I'm not sure how long Joe was in hospital for, or how long he was unconscious, but it must have felt like an eternity for my parents. With the farm work still having to be done and daily visits to their precious little boy, time would have stood still, all the while they had no idea what the outcome for Joe would be.

• CHAPTER 2 •

The Way

I often wonder what went through their minds during that time. Mum was the first child, born when her parents lived in a barn on the property where my grandfather worked as a farm labourer. An idealistic and somewhat fanatical preacher of a small but growing sect of Christians, my grandfather arrived in Australia in 1914 from 'the Old Country' (Great Britain), to preach the Gospel to the lost and 'dying sheep' who'd been deceived by the churches.

Around 1890, William Irvine, who had become disenchanted by the Methodist Church in Scotland, denounced the main churches and stripped his preaching back to the bare basics of Matthew, Mark, Luke and John (the four gospels). I imagine him to have been a very capable speaker, eloquent and full of charisma. He quickly gained followers to what he considered the only 'True Way,' called *The Work*. Initially they stood on street corners converting people, then, "as Jesus sent his disciples two by two," men and women started heading out together to preach this truth, "that came all the way from when Jesus walked on the earth." Either two men or two women together, they spread their 'good news' to England, Ireland and Wales.

My grandfather was born the son of a farmer in County Cary, Ireland, in the late 1800s. People must have been very disenchanted by the conventional churches at that time, because there were many converts all over Great Britain, including my grandfather's family. It was also at the end of the 1800s, when the Brethren (a non-conformist and evangelical Christian movement) sprang up at

Plymouth. In the latter part of the 1800s the Jehovah's Witness and Seventh-day Adventist Church began too. There was a real revival of fundamentalist Christianity around that time, similar to Martin Luther 400 years previously. My grandfather's life became entwined in the movement.

Aged eighteen he enlisted in the Navy, I guess the British, but his zeal to spread the newfound 'truth' was eating at him, so he asked to be discharged from the Navy to work the family farm. This was the only way young men could avoid being, or staying, enlisted.

Upon discharge, he offered to *The Work* to become a preacher of their gospel, *The Way*. He preached in various parts of the British Isles from the age of eighteen, then in 1914 joined a group of several hundred young men and women who embarked on ships set for English-speaking countries. My grandfather was sent to Australia, and preached fervently all over the southern state of Victoria for several years.

With long distances between communities in Australia, he and his companions often found it difficult in a new area. Singing their hymns every evening of the week to the 'strangers' who attended their meetings was proving hard. One of the new converts was a young country lass who had a beautiful singing voice, so I guess Grandad's thinking was that if she accompanied them the singing would be much more attractive.

To do this without the gossip and judgment of the outside world, he married her, only to be told by the 'worker' in charge that it would be best if he now made a home and found a job, as his heart wasn't given wholly to the work of God! And yet, that same 'worker' was married and he and his wife preached together, and they had a little girl, May Carol, who had been brought up by other people so they could continue their work. May was the writer of many of the hymns later included in the movement's hymn book.

The preachers went out preaching, relying solely on gifts from others, the congregation. Thus, when my grandfather left *The Work* he had nothing except his faith, which had been somewhat shaken by being given his marching orders.

The man who married May Carol gave my grandfather a ride

to Queensland in the sidecar of his motorcycle, to the Meaghans, a family north of Brisbane who wanted a farm worker. My grandfather, having been brought up on a farm, was given his first paid job since the Navy. The family stayed good family friends all their lives, and my children now know some of the great grandchildren of that original family. How life weaves its threads. My grandmother arrived later by train to start her married life in the barn, where my mother spent the start of her life. I wonder did Grandad and Grandma feel like Mary and Joseph?

I don't think my mum was treated like Jesus in any way! Just imagine if every baby born into the world was recognized for what they really are, a child of God. Jesus was treated as the son of God from birth. Angels sang, the shepherds and wisemen came with gifts to worship him. The Dalai Lama was revered right from birth as special. If we treated our babies with the same love, reverence and recognition for what and who they truly are, maybe they would grow into similarly gifted beings.

Mum was born a ten-pound baby, and I don't think my poor little grandmother, no taller than five foot, ever forgave her. To my observation, my mum and her mum never really got on well. Conversely, Grandad and my mum were very close all their lives. Mum left home when she was twelve, and from that time on they wrote to each other every week.

· CHAPTER 3 ·

Ethel

"Is that the best you could do, Ethel?" still rings through my head as I write about my grandmother. She particularly loved the twins above me, made obvious by special treats kept especially for them when we visited, which thankfully was very infrequent due to them living in Queensland and us in Tasmania. I can laugh now, but as a little kid it was quite hurtful.

"I love myself for feeling hurt." I say this to myself to recognise and allow the pain. Even as I do so now, I feel a slight ache in my chest.

In response to the ache, I also remember Ho'oponopono, the Hawaiian practice of forgiveness and reconciliation:

> I'm sorry,
> Please forgive me,
> Thankyou,
> I love you.

Born in January 1919, my mum spent most of her first twelve years at Beechmont, up on the ranges above the Gold Coast (Australia), where my grandparents cleared a patch of land that was overrun by lantana on the edge of the rainforest. There they milked a few cows by hand and grew tropical fruit for the local market. From age twelve, Mum went to boarding school at Southport for high school, as the journey then down the ranges to Nerang, to catch the train to Southport, took all day. In contrast, nowadays it's about a forty-five-minute journey by car. So Mum was only home at school holidays, but weekly letter writing kept her in touch with her dad, and maybe there was news of her siblings, George and Viney.

Mum never spoke much of those times, except to say that she would love to have joined in the fun and sports with her schoolmates out of school time. Sadly, I think the matron where she boarded had received orders from her overzealous Christian dad, who wanted his daughter protected at all costs from outside, worldly influences. It would have been extremely lonely. Mum did talk of a time when she went to a friend's place after school, but received such a harsh reprimand she never ventured outside the rules ever again. My poor mum. I wonder how many times she cried herself to sleep? As my mum I never saw her cry, but surely as a young teenager she would have, many times.

I was raised with those same strict Christian guidelines. I remember when television became common in houses, but not ours. Television was believed to be a tool of the devil, thus if we watched it we would be corrupted. I felt terrible guilt when I played at our neighbour's place and we'd go inside and watch cartoons or a western. Their TV faced the window that faced our house, luckily with a good stretch of paddock in between. Their lounge was under that window, and I remember many a time sliding guiltily down so my head wouldn't show out the window where I'd be seen, or rather, caught watching that box that had the power to corrupt my soul.

"I love myself for feeling guilty," I say to myself now, so that all those old patterns will be forever erased from wherever they hide, so no longer may they control my life. In *The Untethered Soul*, Michael A. Singer writes of us having an inner roommate who chats with us, or rather at us, the whole day - our own conditioned thoughts that can make us feel so guilty and ashamed. These two emotions are the worst we can harbor in our bodies. We most often suppress them time and time again to the point they can ruin our health or our lives, giving us cancer or some equally crippling disease. I need to lean into and really feel these emotions even today, love myself for feeling that way, and let them go. That's the way to get my roommate to shut up!

∞

At age seventeen, Mum had completed two years at teachers' college and was assigned her first placement in the education system of Queensland. Situated on the Atherton Tablelands, Ravenshoe Primary School was at least 1000 miles away from home, in the most elevated town in Queensland, and she had thirty-six kids in her first class. In her first year, she had a major fall from her pushbike one frosty, icy morning and sustained a nasty fracture in one knee. She was in a cast with crutches for weeks, and after Grandad's intervention was moved to a school at Victoria Point, near Redland Bay, south of Brisbane.

I imagine Mum must have had a magnetising personality in those days, she was also beautiful and petite, and maintained friendships from those two placements in her first year as a teacher for the rest of her life. She often spoke of and shared letters with us from Stella from Heberton, a town on the tablelands, and the Unwins at Redland Bay won a permanent place in her heart. She would have been yearning for connection during her lonely formative years, then the connections she made when she had the opportunity lasted a lifetime. There was also Betty, one of her earliest colleagues, and Phil (from near Talbot) who she travelled to Tasmania with one Christmas holidays. Phil was originally from Tasmania, and she gets the blame for taking Mum to Gala, the farm near Deloraine, where Dad grew up and where they initially met.

Dad was a shy young bloke and two years younger, so apparently didn't make an impression on Mum's first visit. But he'd seen young Ethel Byrne, and quite a few years later his perseverance would pay off.

Mum spent the rest of her teaching years mainly around the Brisbane area. During the war time she taught during the day and volunteered for signal work during the night. Alf, her then beau, was conscripted and sent to the front, so Mum wanted to become engaged in the war effort to do her part to ensure Alf would return home safely. He never did. Lost in action, he was never heard of again.

During that dreadful time, which in peacetime we can never imagine, Mum burned the candle day and night. That, and the nightmare of not knowing what had happened to the love of her life, became too much. Her mind caved in, and she was committed to the horrifying experience of being locked in an asylum for the mentally ill. Nine months later she was released, I daresay a broken young woman.

Having undergone therapies of the time, which would have included insulin deep sleep therapy, shock treatment, and my mind travels to that chilling old movie, *One Flew Over the Cuckoo's Nest*, I wonder how much of my real mum I ever knew. She went home to the farm to recuperate, and somehow my Dad, who was stationed in Cairns as a medical orderly during the war, had managed to be discharged to work on his future father-in-law's farm. I'm blowed if I know how he managed that one. He had schemed since he was that shy seventeen-year-old!

It is amazing what will transpire when we have a truly burning desire, a dream that we really feel in our body as already having been accomplished. The universe gets behind us, and before we know it our vision becomes a reality. I wonder if Dad had this happen? The higher realms certainly seemed to have his back. I should add he neglected to teach his kids about this phenomenon - his youngest anyway!

· CHAPTER 4 ·

Dad

Dad, the youngest of five children (two girls and three boys), grew up on his parents' dairy farm in an idyllic spot at the foot of Quamby Bluff, south of Deloraine in Tasmania. Pa, his father, was the third child of a migrant school teacher from Scotland who had arrived in Tasmania somewhere around 1875. That was my great grandfather, who I am proud to say received an honourable mention as the headmaster who influenced Frederick Matthias Alexander, founder of the well-known Alexander Technique, when Frederick attended school at Wynyard.

My great-grandfather moved to different schools along the North West of Tasmania, including Forth where I now live, and ended up at Sheffield, where he married a Tasmanian girl (surnamed Wyatt) from around Dunorlan, Mole Creek way. He always referred to her in his writing as Mrs Robertson. He travelled back to Scotland on his own at one stage, by ship as that was the only option in those days. He wrote in his diary, prior to leaving Tasmania, that he had delivered Mrs Robertson to the Wyatt family, where she stayed until he returned. It would have been months later!

While he was teaching in Sheffield, one of their little girls died of Diphtheria (Janet). Soon after the youngest one died also of Diphtheria. Sadly, when my grandfather was three years old both his parents died of Tuberculosis, so he and his older brother and sister were taken in and looked after by their uncle and aunt, who also had a large family of their own. Their family name was Oliver, from the same area near Dunorlan.

Later, when my wife Grada and I lived at Ringarooma with our young family, we visited a young farming couple we got to know. On their mantlepiece was a picture of her grandfather's family when he was young, and there stood my grandfather and his two siblings as well. Amazing, through our kids going to school together I met up with my what would be my third or fourth cousin! There in that little community of Ringarooma, another neighbour turned out to be a grandson of my grandfather's sister, Ann.

I also discovered the wife of the principle of the local high school was a second cousin. I nursed with her at Scottsdale Hospital, and she told me she had visited my grandfather once and always wondered why her family knew nothing about my side of the family tree. They had nothing to do with each other, apparently a rift had separated them when my grandparents had their young family at Quamby Brook.

Prior to 1921, before my dad was born, Pa and Nanna were settling into their little community with their growing family. They were both brought up Church of England. Nanna was a Little by maiden name from Dunorlan, the same community where Pa grew up. They were teenage lovers, and had a courtship that lasted about ten years until Pa could afford his own little farm at Exton. He continued playing cricket for Exton on weekends for social interaction, and attended church on Sundays, but both he and Nanna became increasingly dissatisfied with their life. Cricket was fun when he played, but afterwards he felt flat. Nanna, I guess, was kept busy cooking, cleaning, and looking after the kids, which was the way of the patriarchal society of those times.

There happened to be a couple of the 'workers' preaching in their district, so they went along to listen and felt they made a lot more sense of Christianity than the old church minister offered, plus they seemed to be living according to what was written. After attending the gospel meetings, firstly my grandmother made a choice to leave the church and attend the little home-based meetings that made a revival back in the late 1800s. A year later, Pa, who was always one to sit and observe a while before making up his mind, also quit the church and changed his faith. And that is where the rift occurred. The rest of the family continued with the Church of England and had nothing more to do with Pa and Nanna and their growing family.

Pa's brother had a bit to do with him still, but he didn't have any children. Aunty Ann's family cut them off totally. Religion, religion, religion—we're right, you're wrong. I was brought up the same and I could never understand this need to convert people to our way, although I blindly believed it. My understanding of Jesus' teachings is that as you judge, so will you be judged, and God wants to unite, not divide. All religion has done really is division through judgement of what's right and wrong.

What if there is no right or wrong—it just is! God did say, "I am has spoken," from the verb to be, the same as is!

My dad grew up in a secluded little valley, the youngest of five kids, and learned to be very shy. He told us if he met anyone coming down the road they lived on when he was riding his bike, he'd throw his bike in the bush and hide until they'd gone past. I remember I was shy too, but not quite that shy, only to people I knew. If I met family or people I knew while walking down the street, I'd dash into a shop until they'd gone past. Woe to me if they came into that same shop! Oh boy, "I love myself for feeling shy." I don't know where shyness stems from, maybe from feeling ashamed. "I love myself for feeling ashamed." I really don't know.

Dad went to school until grade seven. The last year he had to ride seven miles (that's about eleven kilometres) into Deloraine to school, then back again at the end of the day. Before and after school the boys also had their share of the milking to do, all by hand. Dad used to tell us stories of his childhood, and it sounded as if they had a lot of fun, especially his brother Bob and him, the youngest boys. They'd play tricks together on their older brother, things like having to go to bed earlier than him and letting off under his pillow and blankets so when he went to bed he'd get gassed, which would end up with them getting woken by a few big thumps from their brother. But boy was it worth it to them! Dad used to still be laughing when he'd tell us.

They were brought up tough and resilient. At seventeen he was left at home on his own to look after the farm for five days. There were no mobile phones in those days, no one to call for help when he developed an excruciating toothache, so Dad hopped on his bike and rode seven miles to the dentist in Deloraine. To prevent that happening ever again, Dad had all his teeth taken out and rode back home again. He had false teeth from that day on.

Dad and his brother used to go hunting all day at times, climbing all over Quamby Bluff following their dogs who chased wallaby scent for miles. They loved their dogs. One of their favourites was poisoned with strychnine once. They used to lay bait laced with strychnine for wallaby, and one day the dog ate a wallaby that had died. So what did the boys do? They bled their dog of poison, cut off the tips of his ears and tail and goodness knows where else, and the poor dog lay around for days but survived, amazingly enough. I don't know what Johanan, my eldest son who is a vet, would say about that treatment, but I sure hope nobody would do such a thing today!

One day my dad's brother, Bob, hid Uncle Ron's new three-legged milking stool up in the top of a tall tree (Ron was the elder brother). Come milking time, Ron couldn't find his new pride and joy anywhere. Eventually he spotted it, and he knew who the culprit was, but Bob was already halfway to a pond to hide behind. Nonetheless, Ron set the chase around and around the pond. Slowly but surely, the gap closed, with Dad and Pa watching on in stitches of laughter. Ron eventually caught him and with some last-ditch effort from pent up anger, he grabbed Bob by the scruff of his neck and the seat of his pants and heaved him as far as he could into the pond.

Apparently, Bob stood up and laughed and laughed. Ron still had to climb the tree to retrieve his stool. A lot of fun was had, usually at someone's expense. Rather a cruel one was at the expense of a crow Dad and Bob had caught somehow. They painted it white and let it go, and much to their glee and horror, they watched as the other crows attacked it and chased it away. So much for colour discrimination only being confined to humans! In between their fun and games, life on the farm kept them busy with an endless supply of often hard manual work.

When the Second World War broke out (1939) my dad and Ron were conscripted, while Bob was allowed to stay and work on the farm 'to feed the nation.' Come parade time in Cairns, North

Queensland, Dad and Uncle Ron refused to carry a rifle. Every morning each would have a firearm thrust at them, accompanied by the barking of the commanding officer, and every morning their firearms clattered to the ground, so strong was their belief in not harming or killing another human being.

Where had that shy, timid youth gone? He would have been only eighteen years old then, but was not to be intimidated. I am proud of my Dad. They were both assigned as medical orderlies. Some of the men they helped treat who were brought back from New Guinea would have made anyone's stomach turn.

When they couldn't get to a little meeting to help keep their faith strong, they would go to a place within the barracks where a weeping tree formed a safe, secret hiding spot where they could meditate alone with their God. Towards the end of the war, Dad managed to be discharged to help on the small patch of cleared lantana at Beechmont, which brought his plan close to fruition. He did have some resistance from family and friends who advised against marrying Mum due to her mental health history, but the stubbornness that let that gun fall rattling to the ground time after time stood him in good stead. His love and loyalty never wavered.

∞

Before long they were home in Tasmania with their second child on the way, while standing over their first little boy as he lay in hospital, and wondering why such a terrible thing had happened.

"Take him home and treat him as a normal child," the doctor told them, as if he was damaged beyond repair. What a heartbreak that must have been! Needless to say, the horse at fault was quickly sent to the knackers for pet food at rather a big loss for the young fledgling farmers. Being the youngest in a family of seven kids, I didn't really get to hear a lot about the next part of family history. It seemed I was a generation younger than my oldest brother, Joe, so I didn't get to know him as I did my other siblings. A few months after bringing him home, "to treat him as a normal child," Rob was born, who legend has it didn't smile until he was a year old.

You can't tell me babies in utero don't experience feelings or emotions. Rob would have had all the chemicals my mum was producing from the shock and trauma of Joe's injury coursing through his little body for the last few months of pregnancy. Something had certainly suppressed his happy hormones. At one year old he started smiling, and hasn't stopped since. You know how there's usually a joker in every family, well Rob is ours. He could turn the mood around in our house and have us all laughing at the drop of a hat.

As for Joe, I must say I've never known Joe as 'not a normal person.' He must have been about sixteen when we moved to Sprent. He'd just completed High School with flying colours, and I have it in my head he became Dux of Devonport High School. I may be wrong, but either way there seemed to be no apparent injury to his brain. Many years later he was involved in a car accident, resulting in him having a CT scan of his head. Lo and behold they discovered some major trauma had been inflicted on his brain, but it was old. The only other time was when he was one-year-old. If scientists had studied his brain from the accident at one-year-old onward, they would have discovered the plasticity of the brain years before, and our amazing ability to heal and for the brain to develop new pathways. My parents never once entertained the fact that his brain was anything but normal. Their faith, belief and thoughts made him whole.

· CHAPTER 5 ·

Brothers

Anyway, back to me and my fish.

After spending the best part of a week celebrating my first fish that I caught all by myself (well, almost), I was able to go to our new family home. I'm not sure what time of year it was, but life on a farm seems to always be busy. The new farm was more than twice the size of my parents' first farm, so the milking herd increased, and during the winter months I would often pester my father to go with him to feed the cows.

Gloves mustn't have been thought of in those days, that or the dollars didn't quite stretch that far. I also remember shorts and bare feet in gumboots were the order of the day, and my oh my, the winter seemed a mighty lot colder in those days too! I'd cling to the metal bar on the carryall, desperately trying not to cry from the pain in my frozen fingers as we bounced our way all over the farm, feeding hay to the heifers, dry cows, and some to the bulls.

I remember time after time I'd go into the bathroom on returning home to run warm water over my frozen hands to thaw them. I'd cry with the pain of the blood returning to the extremities, then I'd repeat it the next day, and the next. There was far more excitement feeding out than being cramped up inside with all the other kids at school. Even so, I would ask my parents day after day, "When can I go to school? Surely I can go to school now?"

When I was five, a year or so after moving to the Sprent farm, Mum was taking her usual nap after lunch while Dad was busy outside. The weather must have been ok, so I set off to school by myself. I was about a kilometre away from the school, it was in plain sight, when I saw the bus coming towards me. The yellow canary, as it was called, swooped down on me and kept racing past, oblivious to the little boy shyly waving for it to stop. I think I may have started crying, when I heard a kind lady's voice asking whether I was ok.

It was Mrs Bennett, the mother of Julie, who would be in my class the following year. She gently guided me to her car and took me home to the rousing welcome of my twin brothers' ridicule. My parents were oblivious to the fact that I had disappeared for a couple of hours. What an adventure for those little legs, and oh to return to the safety of those times when there was no danger for children walking along country roads, where neighbours looked out for each other.

I loved school from the day I started. At home I was the underdog to twin brothers. They were almost three years older than me and I so wanted them to include me. I guess I was a little nuisance brother to them, but I didn't realise that at the time and mostly just felt left out. So I couldn't understand kids crying when they were dropped off at school, there I was an equal with my peers, I was included—all day long!

School was exciting and I was eager to learn. I still remember receiving a book as first prize in grade one as if it was yesterday. I think what remains of the book, *The Three Little Pigs*, is still included with the kids' books on the shelves for our grandkids. Even now I can feel that sense of pride at presentation night.

During those first few years at school I saw my brothers in a different light. I didn't have to fear anyone at school, only the teachers and headmaster, because if any bigger kid tried to pick a fight with me they had both my twin brothers, Winston and James, to contend with. Needless to say, I was left well alone by the school bullies.

My nickname was Pepper, supposedly because I could get a bit hot under the collar. At home I needed to at times when my brothers' protection turned to teasing, and often bullying at its worst. I remember many a time being held down by one while the other held the face of a gorilla from a geographic magazine close to my face. I would scream, utterly terrified by the face. My squeals mainly went unheeded because they always carefully chose a place out of earshot of Mum, and Dad was usually outside working. I often wonder how I would have gone assisting Jane Goodall doing her research on the big silverbacks, I would have had to face my demons.

I couldn't eat the same things the rest of the family did if it was made with milk, but living on a dairy farm, milk was a main staple. As a baby, after Mum stopped breastfeeding me and I started on other milk, I would just throw it back up. Same with goat's milk. Mum sought help, but no one had heard of a baby being intolerant to all types of milk and the doctors and nurses had no suggestions. Watching her little baby fade away from malnourishment, my mum became resourceful. She had read that Arabs fed their horses dates for a good iron supply, and being brought up herself in Queensland where bananas grew plentifully, she started me on a diet of dates, bananas and fruit juices for liquids. To this day I still love dates and bananas.

So of course when I was given my special food it seemed to my siblings as if I was being spoiled, especially when dessert came along, which was often junket, even though they didn't really enjoy it. Junket was a tablet that set or curdled slightly warmed milk, a bit like custard but not really. I often wondered whether that made my older twin brothers jealous, because there were often times when they really hated my guts. One would taunt and tease while the other looked on and laughed, then the other would take over.

I wonder what protective mechanisms this instilled in my personality? If we did perchance play nicely together, they would often run away and hide, leaving me alone, sometimes a long way from the safety of the house. I remember many a time crying my way home, feeling scared out of my wits. Looking back there was nothing to be scared of, but in the imaginative brain of a small boy who had been fed stories from older brothers, there was a wolf or gorilla waiting to pounce from behind every blade of grass.

I made some good friends at school, one boy especially, Rod Stevens from across the valley. We spent lots of Saturdays together, hunting rabbits with ferrets and nets. I'd often yell out to Mum as I raced out the door, "Just going to Rod's," not waiting for an answer in case it was no. I'd jump the fence across the road at the end of our drive and run across the farm paddocks, across the wall of a big dam catching the flow of the creek for irrigation, then up the hill another half kilometre to Rod's house. You could see it from our place, but it was over on what we called the main road.

Quite often it'd be after school, just in time for the cartoons or a good western on TV, which further built up my guilt that I'd be struck down because it was evil. The old phone on the wall would ring. It was one you had to ring the handle six times or so to wake the lady at the exchange or give her time to run back from putting the veggies on for tea. Then she'd connect your line with whoever you wanted to speak to, all the time able to eavesdrop on any conversation. What a minefield of information, or rather gossip, the exchange lady must have been! "Did you hear that blah, blah, blah!"

Politeness was everything. I clearly remember being told off by Dad, rather harshly and unjustly I thought. Our neighbour, Mr Wood, was in a hurry on his little tractor one day, tearing across the paddock next door to us. Dad and three of my brothers and I were in the cow yard for some reason, the twins and I clinging to the top metal rail while standing two rails up. We all laughed at seeing the little grey Fergie tractor bounce and career over the cattle ruts in the paddock.

"Give it to her, Henry!" I yelled out, causing more laughter from my brothers, but not from Dad. He glared at me and almost shouted at me never to talk like that again or refer to Mr Wood as Henry. Everyone knew him as Henry, but in those days we were expected to refer to our elders as Mr or Mrs. My older brothers working on the farm referred to him as Henry, so it seemed unfair and harsh, spoiling the moment of us all having a good laugh together. Maybe Dad felt guilty at laughing at Henry's expense and took it out on me. It made a big impression on me anyway, and even as an adult married to Grada, I'd often refer to people as Mr and Mrs, and even 'be polite' when saying hello, calling them Mr and Mrs. Grada would look at me with a questioning look. How times have changed.

Looking up at Mrs Stevens, Rod's mum, I'd wait for her to look and smile. A beautiful, gentle lady, who I had never even considered calling anything but Mrs Stevens, she'd just say, "Time for tea." I'd back slowly out the door to catch as much of the story in the western as possible, you see that call usually came at a really exciting time.

Once out the door I'd turn and run as quickly as I could over the paddock, across the dam and up the hill to our place, careful not to catch skin or clothes on the barbed wire as I crept through or over the fences. I'd run especially fast if the sun was down and darkness was creeping across the valley. I think my heart thumped more from fear than the exertion of the run, fear of that boogeyman lurking in the shadows. What if my twin brothers were right after all?

• CHAPTER 6 •

Language

Growing up on the farm we had a lot of fun. If we wanted something special to make the fun with we either had to make it ourselves, or make the money to buy it, which made us very resourceful. We charged Mum money for the rabbits we caught, for we could have otherwise sold them to the butcher in town for forty cents a pair. We'd catch the rabbit, either trapping or with ferrets and nets, then deliver a quick karate chop or twist of the neck to end its life, quickly followed by a slit in the throat to bleed (the meat was inedible if you didn't bleed them).

We learned from a young age how to do that, because if you wanted the money, you had to do the work. Skinning, cleaning the gut and cutting off the feet and head wasn't pleasant, but rabbits were considered pests. Originally brought to Australia from England with the first white settlers, they soon spread right across our country.

Grada was taught at school in Holland that the rabbits who threatened to undermine the dykes and dunes that keep the sea out were originally introduced from Australia! I laughed when she told me that, as the rabbit is certainly not one of our native animal species and has wreaked havoc across Australia. An extremely long fence was built—thousands of miles across the Red Centre of mainland Australia—to stem the tide of the rabbits spreading across the continent. In country Tasmania, my brothers and I were glad of the little rabbit to make our pocket money from.

Saturdays we'd go all day. Rod would bring his ferret and I'd take one or two of ours. Every farm boy seemed to have ferrets in those days. We'd head down across the farm in search of their burrows, which were better than stone heaps because you could place a net over the entrance and send the ferret down the burrow, scaring the unsuspecting bunny so it would run straight out and into our nets. Sometimes we'd spend a frustrating afternoon waiting for the ferret to re-emerge, as he would have caught a rabbit in a dead-end somewhere, had a big feast and gone to sleep. We'd be stamping all over the paddock trying to wake him up. Sometimes we'd go home and get a shovel and dig him out, following the burrow until we found him.

Usually he'd stretch and yawn, blinking in the bright daylight as if to say, "Excuse me, but you're disturbing my siesta." We'd keep the rabbits alive in a hessian sack until we got home, where we could kill, bleed, skin and gut them in that order. Our emotions didn't seem to get in the way at all as we looked into those innocent eyes, pleading with us in fear of their imminent death. It was just a job to be done.

In the stone heaps where they lived, we had less chance to catch them because they had multiple places to enter and leave. The stone heaps were huge piles of big and small rocks picked up from the paddocks that we cultivated for cropping. There was a never-ending supply. Each year the ground was ploughed there were more rocks, and guess who had to pick them up so they wouldn't damage any farm implements - yours truly and my older brothers.

Some stones were so huge it took two or three of us to lift them. On to the trailer they went, to then be tipped on the ever-growing mountains, usually on an area of the farm that was unproductive, and sometimes they were used to fill creek beds to make a roadway. Anyway, they provided great refuge for the vulnerable little bunnies who came out at night to eat all the valuable grass meant for the milking cows. All that backbreaking lifting didn't seem to do us any harm. I don't think any of us suffered too much and it was free bodybuilding - no gym needed for boys on the farm. There was also no time to go into town anyway!

When my grandkids read this they'll be utterly disgusted at their Pap's lack of feeling and compassion I'm sure. Anyway, we'd stretch the skins out on a wire frame and hang them on a sheltered side of the shed for the sun to dry them. Every so often a man would come around the farms and buy the skins. If Dad had killed any sort of animal for meat for the kitchen table, be it a sheep or steer, the skin was sold to the tanner to bring in a little extra cash for family expenses. Our rabbit skins helped weigh our pockets down with a few extra coins as well, that was until we could get into town to spend it.

There were special times throughout the year that deserved our money being spent. Christmas was one, where everyone in the family bought presents for everyone else. It truly was an exciting time. I can remember going with Mum when I was young, then later on my own. With nine people to buy for in our large family we probably learned to budget early in life, at least in a small way.

"How much is this?" Count the pennies. Would it leave enough for something for that last present I had to get? Then there were birthdays. Nine of those a year. My sister Marg's birthday was just before Christmas, and she often complained it wasn't fair because her birthday and Christmas tended to be lumped into one. I don't blame her really.

Marg was the only girl with six brothers. To her life wasn't fair, but to us boys she seemed to have the life of privilege. We had to do jobs outside and help with the farm work, plus take our turn washing and wiping up after meals, while Marg didn't seem to have to do much and she made sure we had to do our share of that. We were often cruel, calling her Madam Muck of Turd Island. It would have been a bit of a lonely existence for her in a male-dominated family.

And yet, Marg was patient and loving towards her younger brothers, always. I remember when she lived in Melbourne there was always a bed or a sofa to bunk on for a night or two, with meals supplied. We often arrived at short notice, but Marg never said, "No, sorry, you can't stay." She and Rob were always close and have lived near each other most of their lives. Even as I write, Rob is building a new home in Daylesford, Victoria, where Marg lives.

∞

In primary school I was popular, the head of the group, a good scholar and a good runner, the fastest in my grade. Unfortunately, Mum and Dad didn't encourage us to play sport, as that led to weekend sporting activities which were 'worldly' and took peoples' attention away from God. I did play footy and cricket a bit with the school team, but only during school time and practice after school was not allowed.

Once in grade five, a team for cricket was to be chosen to play against other schools. Every boy in the class wanted to be on that team picked from grade five and six boys. The captain, who was in grade six and the best cricket player at the time, had to choose his team. It was an anxious time of anticipation. At the end of the week my name wasn't on the team. I took it to heart and sought him out on the playground during a break to ask why he hadn't chosen me.

"Because you're not good enough."

I was angry.

I remember quite plainly I swore for the first time in my life. I called him a C**T. I may have put the adjective of bloody in front of it as well, I can't remember that detail. What plagued me for days, months, maybe even years later, was guilt at having called him those words. I can't remember having my mouth washed out with soap and water ever, but to swear was bad, and I had been taught that God heard and saw everything we did.

That feeling of guilt that religion causes, even in lives so young, is immense and crazy. I can remember drilling that same dogma into my own kids, much to my shame when I think of it now. Suppressed guilt supposedly has an energetic vibration similar to that of death!

I heard a story of a little boy walking into a butcher's shop with his parents, years ago, during the hippy era. Anyway, when the little bloke watched the butcher cut up an animal on his bandsaw and cut through the carcass with the knife, he said to the butcher that he was, "bloody cruel," and, "a fucking murderer." His parents didn't blink an eyelid, but all the other customers and the butcher were shocked to the back teeth. The little boy had no guilt or shame around using those adjectives. I'm not sure why the parents took him in there, maybe as part of his education of human psychology!

I can still feel the guilt I felt all those years ago, when I was eleven years old and calling my school mate those words, yet that little boy was as happy as Larry, with no feelings blocking the joy in his life. He was just stating his truth.

• CHAPTER 7 •

Life Learning

The older I got the more I understood that life on a farm was hard work, and the harder the work became. How we played changed as we grew too. Us younger three boys were adventurous, on rainy days we'd play in the barn, making forts and tunnels in among the hay bales, often making several rooms joined by tunnels. Then we'd play hide and seek. It was as dark as night in the forts, especially in the tunnels, so you could stay hidden for what seemed like hours. I remember sometimes I'd be out and had to seek, then my brothers would quietly sneak back to the house, leaving me trying to find them for ages until I gave up and went back to the house myself, only to find them laughing and enjoying a hearty afternoon tea.

Hay was made in the summer and fed to the cattle during the cold and wet winter months. Often Dad would think he had heaps of hay left and start giving a little bit more to fatten the cows, only to discover several big holes in the stack where our forgotten forts had been. He was never cross or angry at us, I imagine he and his brother Bob had most likely done the same thing forty years earlier at Quamby Brook.

The hay was made during December, usually after the grass had grown to well over a couple of feet tall. Mainly rye grass, it was bliss lying down in the long grass and playing hide and seek with each other and the dogs. We had to make sure to stay well away from the tractor and the mower though. The dogs often went extremely close to the razor-sharp blades that whizzed back and forth as the grass was laid down in neat rows across the field.

The grass had alternating seed heads all up the stem. We would often lay in the warm summer sun, soaking up its heat after the chilly winter, pulling off seed after seed as we said, "Tinker, tailor, soldier, sailor, rich man, poor man, beggar man, thief," all the way to the last seed, and whatever the last one ended up on, that's what we'd become! Needless to say, there was always a fair bit of cheating to make it end up on, "rich man." If only we'd realised then how rich we were.

We'd help cart the hay into the barn with tractor and trailer. Usually it was the hottest part of the year and the sweat would soak our t-shirts front and back. Lucky for us, Dad had built a huge reservoir right beside the sheds on the highest part of the farm for farm, house and dairy use. Between loads it was a quick skinny dip to cool off, with the dogs yapping at us furiously from the bank. Often one would join us, swimming from one side to the other faster than we could.

One day we heard the older dog barking over near the dam and went to investigate. There was a young dog swimming as fast as he could, chasing a family of native hens swimming on the dam, while the older dog ran around the outside, keeping the native hens in the water. Bruce, the young dog, had his work cut out. He'd swim towards one, which would then dive under water. He'd turn and chase another, then that one would dive. He didn't have a chance, the poor bloke, so the twins and I stripped off and helped him in the chase. We actually caught five out of the six. One older hen managed to escape. We were certainly puffed, but felt triumphant.

Mum was keen to try a native hen stew, so they were gutted and cleaned, ready for the pot. Story has it that if you want to eat native hen, you hang it up in a tree in a bag with a stone. After a week you put both the hen and the stone in the pot and boil for a few hours, then you take out the bird, throw it away and eat the stone. If you've ever seen a native hen, they are very lean. Not a skerrick of fat, and very sinewy. All five birds went in the pot. There were four young ones that were quite tender after a few hours, the older one went to the dogs! They deserved it for their part in the hunt.

I thought my life was lonely, it certainly seemed that way in my early teens. When I went to high school life changed. Most of my friends from Sprent School went on to Devonport High School, while only three of us went to Ulverstone High. It depended very much on the bus runs. Rod (my mate on the main road) and I went to Ulverstone, along with Sally, whose family had moved to Gawler.

I was one kid among a thousand students at that school, feeling very alone, and I became shy and withdrawn. I seemed to stand out like a sore thumb. Long hair was in for boys in the 70s after the Beatles rocked the world and the hippies were in full swing, but according to the church, and therefore my parents, it was of the devil. Short back and sides was the uniform, no long hair or beards for boys or men, and hair done up in a bun for the women. Rob, my brother who didn't smile until he was one but had now become the joker of the family, dared to be different. He sported a beard. His disobedience earned him his marching orders - he was excommunicated from the church!

I was very self-conscious with my short back and sides, being ridiculed and feeling very alone, yet somehow I was still convinced we were the only ones going to Heaven. The church convinced us that everyone else was lost forever and they would end up in Hell. And yet, I dared not be seen by my peers with my tie on going to a gospel meeting. I would have rather died. I dared not speak one word of my family's beliefs.

I was just shy. That is what I believed anyway. I found it very hard to make any new close friends and my friendship with Rod seemed to end there, after we were sorted into different groups or levels according to our academic results. I was placed in a totally different class than Rod, with me going into maths and science and Rod heading to the technical classes. Within our group of family and friends within the church, I had no one I was close to, no one my own age. There were kids two to three years older and younger. Even at our convention, which I thoroughly enjoyed as a child, there wasn't anyone I really connected with.

Towards the end of my second year of high school, Mum and Dad decided they needed to go and look after my grandparents in

Queensland. I was too young to leave at home with my brothers, I think my eldest brother Joe was looking after the farm. The twins were in their matriculation year at high school (the last year before university), so they couldn't be uprooted for the last six weeks of school prior to their end exams. So, it was me travelling with Mum and Dad, although I'm not sure why we went as Grandma was as cantankerous as ever and couldn't stand my mother doing anything for her.

While we were living with my grandparents I went to Wynnum High School, where I was put into first year, which is year eight in Queensland. The subjects were slightly different, but I managed to fit in and learned well, gaining good marks at the end of the year. I remember being befriended by some of the kids in the class, but again there was no intermingling or sport after school due to them being 'not one of us,' not sharing our beliefs.

Thus, again, I felt very alone. However, I stood out as the shy little boy from Tasmania, so at school I did develop some friendships. It was in some of the airy outside corridors of the school on stilts that my sex education began, with some bewilderment on my behalf. My 'friends' began fondling and groping one another in places I was totally green about.

Back home at Grandma and Grandad's a bath before bed in about two inches of water became my refuge, until there was a loud tapping on the door.

"What are you doing in there?"

"No more than two inches of water please!"

Grandad's voice, but I could hear Grandma egging him on. At an age where life revolved around me and my somewhat lonely existence, I was too young to be concerned about what they had lived through. They had survived two world wars and the Depression (1920s-1930s), scratching a living from the land, and having to battle ever encroaching rainforest to have enough grass for their cows. Perhaps not an ideal place for cows, but that was probably all they knew.

Dad tells the story of when he was discharged from the Army to work on their farm at Beechmont. Uncle George (Mum's brother) and Dad were milking the cows, by hand of course. No electricity there in those days, let alone milking machines. Grandma was keeping a watchful eye on the young men to make sure they were doing it properly. They let one cow out after milking and Grandma was adamant they hadn't milked her properly. They assured her they had, but Grandma's Scottish nature was far from satisfied. She chased the cow back into the stall, squatted beside her and vigorously attempted to extract more milk from her apparently empty udder. Eventually, to her satisfaction, she ended up with a cupful of extra milk! I guess that would have fed a hungry belly during those hard times.

Anyway, that scarcity mindset didn't leave her until the day she died, along with the stubbornness of the bravest Scot that ever lived. Luckily, I didn't have to rely on the water to keep me warm in the bath, as for me bath time was also an escape from the muggy Queensland heat. I simply lay in the cool water, trying not to hear the muttering behind the door.

Come school holidays the twins arrived from Tasmania, and lo and behold out came the White Christmas treat that I'd only been allowed to look at in the fridge, causing my salivary glands to work overtime. After the twins were offered a piece, or it may have been two pieces that was pushed into their hands, the plate was returned to the fridge. I hadn't seen Grandma look so happy the whole time I'd been there. It was her favourite little boys, now strapping seventeen-year-olds, who'd brought about the change.

They were still her cuties, and me, I was still, "Is that the best you could do, Ethel?"

My sister Marg, and her friend Liz, came and spent a few weeks holiday as well. I'm not sure where everyone slept, it must have been a nightmare for Grandma. I consoled myself in the fact that Liz showered me with some overdue love and attention, even though I was a little nuisance to her. I hadn't come across women shaving their legs before. I'd touch her legs where bristles had started to grow again and go, "ouch," pretending they had stuck into my fingers. Very mean actually, but she endured me with good humour and gave me attention I'd longed for in my loneliness.

Towards the end of the school holidays my parents decided they'd had enough abuse from an ungrateful old lady and we all headed home to Tasmania.

Whenever I smell tomatoes, brushing beside them in the garden or hothouse, it reminds me of that time with my grandparents. During our stay, my dad had gotten some part-time work on a market garden at Rochedale picking tomatoes, and I'd go with him and help pick if I wasn't at school. It was the time of year when the monsoon season had just begun, so about 3 o'clock nearly every afternoon, a cloud would burst with a few claps of thunder and we'd race for shelter. One afternoon we really had to race for our lives. It started hailing what looked like golf balls, with some stones even like tennis balls. If one had hit us on the head it would have quite easily knocked us out. Car roofs and bonnets were terribly dented and the loss to the market gardeners with stripped vines brought Dad's employment to an abrupt halt.

Another time I was with Marg and Rob on holiday in Queensland, when I was nearly twelve. We were visiting friends near Gympie (and their daughter Maggie, who was about Rob's age), and had to cross over the Mary River. It was just a tiny stream with the bridge way above - it looked ridiculous. I asked our friends why, and they said sometimes the water goes above the bridge. No, that was unbelievable.

We were to stay the weekend. I now know that the people we stayed with were probably prearranged with great care, as Rob and Marg were getting to the age where they were interested in the opposite sex, so the need for a holiday at places where there were 'nice' girls and boys of the same fellowship is obvious. I think now our parents sent me as a chaperone so they wouldn't go too wild away from home. It must have been terrible for them to have me tagging along.

That weekend it started to rain. And rain.

The bridge was well and truly under water, and we were stuck there for ten days, not just a weekend. All week it rained. The cane toads barked like dogs outside our windows, the clothes in our cases went mouldy, and somehow Maggie remained just a friend!

Later on that trip, back down through New South Wales and Victoria, we stayed with the Morris family near Mildura, Gol Gol actually. Ruth, one of their nine children, had done her midwifery training at Devonport and visited our place frequently, frequently enough for a romance to begin to flourish with Joe, my eldest brother. Rob was a bit of a larrikin and played the piano accordion. The piece he played especially for Ruth was aptly named *Old black Joe.* While we were there a storm of another nature arrived, big rolling clouds of dust blown in from the desert blotted out the afternoon sun. Quickly, all the windows were closed and shuttered, with towels and blankets blocking cracks, but nothing could keep out the fine brown dirt of inland Australia.

Thus, after the mould of Queensland, our clothes were then full of the dust of Mildura. I eventually arrived home well after school had begun for the year. All my teachers said when my parents explained that I would be home a week late was, "He'll learn a lot more than whatever I could teach him," and I daresay I did. Experiencing the awesomeness of nature first-hand could never be learned in a classroom.

• CHAPTER 8 •

Mike

Back to high school at Ulverstone and into grade nine, I slotted into my old groove. I did my schoolwork, and had crushes on girls a couple of grades below, so safe enough for me. What did eventuate that year was the start of a strong and lasting friendship in my life. Geoff, my cousin and the same age as my twin brothers, asked if I wanted to go to the North East of Tasmania to a family within our church for the May school holidays.

Yes, I was allowed to go, and what a balm to my soul. Mike Jones was my age and a lot of fun, we hit it off from day one. Why I hadn't met him at our annual church convention, I'll never know. I couldn't be more grateful to Geoff for taking me there. The Jones family became my second family, and from those holidays on, I was either at Ringarooma visiting Mike, or Mike was at my place. He was the joker in his family, making everyone laugh. How I wish I could remember more of those times!

Ringarooma was the edge of the wild west, or so it seemed to me. We'd ride motorbikes and horses, and spent hours building a secret little fort for ourselves, hidden by trees and perching on the fence of an elderly neighbour's garden. That is where we would go to dream. It was also where I nearly coughed my lungs out after trying my first cigarette (Mike had older cousins who were able to acquire them for him). It was exciting, eating the forbidden fruit.

I remember one holidays when Mike and Bob (Mike's cousin the same age) came to stay. We'd go riding or rambling all over the countryside. We had an old cut-down Ford Prefect car, Joe's first car that he had donated to his younger siblings—probably because it wasn't worth anything! It consisted of the engine sitting on a shortened chassis with one bench seat, four wheels and a steering wheel. We'd go all over the farm in it, and along a pretty rough pipeline access road to the Gawler River, where we'd fish until dark. Often we'd stay until well after dark and fish for the blackfish that came out at night. We'd always be in luck.

During the day, sometimes we'd catch a sick old rabbit, tie it on to baling twine and dangle it in the river. This was before the old freshwater lobsters were protected. One would grab hold of the rabbit for a feed and we'd simply haul him in, careful not to get our fingers close to those dark, cold, prehistoric claws that were strong as vices. Once those claws closed you couldn't open them, the lobster wouldn't let go of his dinner. Instead, he'd be dinner for the whole family. The same as crayfish, only freshwater. I think we'd gone past the age of charging Mum for our catches at that stage. Mind you, we always filled the old car up from the farm's fuel tank with not a word of complaint from Dad, so I reckon we owed a lot more than we gave by the time we left home. I read somewhere that it costs about $230,000 to raise a child to age seventeen—on the cheap! No wonder my parents didn't get out of the red until they sold the farm when I was about eighteen. Seven times $230,000—they could have been millionaires. I'll have to remind my kids of this!

Quite often we'd drive up a laneway from the back of our farm on to the road about a mile from our drive. We'd look up and down the road, then if nothing was coming, we'd take off at top speed, which in modern cars would have been only about 50km/hour, hoping no police would come around the corner between us and our driveway. We managed to avoid detection pretty well every time, except once when I drove the 'old bomb' as we called it down our lane to get the mail. Our box was on the opposite side of the road to our drive, so I'd do a big sweep and pull up beside the box so I didn't have to get off the seat. I don't think it had a handbrake, anyway.

I was just reaching into the box one day and around the corner came Constable Innes. He was in his old jeep, off duty, but he pulled up and asked what I was doing on the road, and said he'd be back later to talk to Dad. I drove back up the drive to the house, parked the car and was nearly pooping myself for the rest of the day, waiting for Constable Innes to return. After a couple of days he hadn't returned, and I tossed caution to the wind again. When I went for my driver's licence the day I turned seventeen, have a guess who took me for my test. You guessed, Constable Innes.

"Well, I know you can drive alright, but let's see if you know your rules," he said as he hopped in beside me. Away we went. The speed limits had recently been altered in towns from thirty-five miles per hour to sixty kilometres per hour (that's about thirty-seven miles per hour). So that's telling my age! Our car still had miles per hour on the gauge, so me being me (you ask Grada!) I drove all through town doing thirty-seven miles per hour. We arrived back at the station and everything had gone ok, I thought!

"There's one thing," he said.

My heart galloped into my throat, like it does whenever the cops pull you up.

"Just mind your speed."

I almost said, "But I wasn't speeding," but was wise enough to keep my mouth shut! Phew.

Prior to getting my car licence, I'd persuaded Dad he needed a little motorbike for on the farm, and just in case we went on the road we'd better register it. That's how at sixteen I got my learner's licence, which included motorbike. The kilometres I travelled on that little 100cc Suzuki bike were amazing. To and from school, back and forth to Ringarooma. I was free at last—oh what a feeling!

∞

Those trips to Ringarooma were the best. Fun, laughter, adventure and excitement, and a real friend at last. We'd explore old mine shafts in the bush around the rugged hills surrounding Ringarooma, we'd fish and hunt, and set snares for possums. Skins supplemented our pocket money very nicely.

Ringarooma was a very fertile little farming community, almost completely surrounded by rugged mountain ranges and state forest. Later, Grada and I would move there to give our children what we thought would be an idyllic lifestyle.

As teenagers, Mike and I were young and fearless, making the most of every moment we were alive. Mike had left school after year ten to work on the farm with his dad, who was in partnership with his brother, Bob. Mike had to milk their ever-increasing herd of cows morning and night, then help his Dad feed pigs, and then shift irrigation with Tanya, an amazon of a local woman.

Tanya worked to support a large family while her husband whiled his time away, mostly leaning on the bar at the pub. He was a measly little character. We often wondered why Tanya put up with him, she could have snapped his neck with one hand if she wanted to. She was a larger than life, jovial lady, always happy, or so it seemed, even laughing as she carried twice the number of irrigation pipes that Mike or I could across the rough potato mounds. At harvest time she could pick up more potatoes in a day than any young, able-bodied man, bending all day without complaint. With a heart of gold, she was a joy to spend the time of day with, even if it was hard yakka.

Tim, Mike's dad, had lots of people on his casual labour list. They'd come and go a bit, it seemed as if they'd go walkabout every now and then. Peter was one young bloke who springs to mind. He was taken in by Tanya and sheltered from a fairly rough upbringing. Ringarooma was a very isolated community in earlier times, and I guess poverty mixed with the pub being the only social outing for blokes led to some families being quite under-privileged, with alcohol lending its hand to violence. But such were those particular out-of-the-way communities.

You couldn't say there wasn't a community spirit. People such as Tanya, and Tim and Mary (Mike's parents), would often take in the strays who had fled an unhappy home life. The open fire was always going to warm bodies coming in chilled to the bone from frost, wind and rain. The kettle was forever hot for a cuppa, with fresh scones from the oven with jam and cream or an overflowing plate of roast meat and veggies, which equally warmed from the inside.

"What's for dinner Mary?" I don't know how many times that

question rang out as stragglers came in from the farm. Often, they came hours apart from their different chores. Food was always ready and a good hot cuppa in front of you before you had time to wash and sit down.

The patience of an angel and the grace and love of what we'd equate to God. That was Mary. Beautiful through and through. She eventually died of stomach cancer, a horrible way for such a beautiful lady to go.

As young daredevils, Mike and I were oblivious to any underlying issues lurking in the shadows. We would often go spotlighting at night, shooting and chasing kangaroos and wallabies that were forever encroaching on the pasture that was meant to be turned into milk. They were classified as a pest to be got rid of. Those excursions often led us to Mathinna and Upper Esk, the back of beyond. Up over the highland Mathinna Plains, racing along forestry tracks at breathtaking pace, we felt so alive!

· CHAPTER 9 ·

Connections

Stuart, a young bloke from Victoria who'd initially come and worked for Tim, had bought a marginal farm at the head of a valley at Upper Esk to strike out on his own. He had a small herd of cows and spent long, backbreaking hours clearing bush and building his own dairy, milking the cows, and feeding his pigs. He supplemented his meagre income by cutting and carting hop poles for the hop fields around Scottsdale.

Some evenings, or you could say most nights, Stuart would stagger in, hoping his slow combustion stove that supplied his hot water was still alight and burning. He'd trim an old kerosene lamp or light a candle, warm up some leftovers, or quickly cook a chop or omelette on the stove, then run the bath and lie in the luxurious steaming water to relieve his aching muscles. He'd be so exhausted that many times he'd wake up stiff with the cold, a black coating of grime floating on top of the once warm bath water. If you saw his neck and the side of the bath there was nearly always a dirty black ring all the way around.

Later, Stuart married a lass from Launceston and they had five children, including twin boys. Grada and I visited a few times, they were a happy young family. The power had been connected by then, luckily for Sue with five little kids. Even so, you could tell life was taking its toll on her in that lonely, out of the way piece of paradise.

I think it was about 1989, when I was in my second year of nursing training in Launceston, that I was told the horrifying news.

One of the nurses in my group was Chris, who grew up on the next farm to Stuart and Sue. I was doing my stint of training in theatre with Chris when she received a call from her parents to say Stuart, who had continued to supplement the family income with hop poles, had been killed in an accident.

Stuart was travelling towards Launceston with his loaded truck when he met an empty log truck that was speeding towards him on the narrow country road. He had to get out of its way. Moving off to the side, he didn't see the culvert pipe that his front left wheel abruptly fell in. Stuart and his truck came to a sudden halt, but the momentum kept the poles he was carting travelling forward though the cab. The poor guy didn't have a hope.

Sue was left in that Godforsaken place on her own, with five little kids to raise. Luckily, she was able to sell the property, and Stuart had left a good insurance in case of that precise thing happening, but all the money in the world could never replace the life of your partner. This was the second major devastating blow to the Jones family in about nine years, as they'd considered Stuart as a son and brother.

Mike and I had loved going to Stuart's, and he seemed to enjoy our visits just as much. Often, we'd go with a group of young people, all piled in, and on the back of a couple of four-wheel drive Land Rovers, with rifles and guns in hand. Spotlights on each vehicle, we'd carefully circumnavigate the paddocks close to the bush-line in search of wallabies. Sure enough, head after head would pop up to look at us, still chewing Stuart's precious grass that was meant for his cows. The echo of gunshots reverberated around the hills for what seemed like minutes. The poor little wallabies, dazzled by the bright spotlights, didn't have a hope. Often, they'd start hopping straight towards us.

Mike being the clown he was, would often bang on the roof for the driver to stop. Then he'd jump off and chase the blinded wallaby to catch him by the tail. The wallaby would then make a colossal effort to escape Mike's grip. We'd be falling off the tray of the Land Rover from laughing as we watched Mike being jerked this way and that, ever slowly into the bush. Many times, the whole party would join in the chase and experience the joy of joltingly being pulled through the cow muck that had been left to cool by the herd the day before. Or we'd crash into dead branches and trees lying in our way, all of which the wallaby could so cunningly avoid.

We'd return exhausted to Stuart's house, crank up the teapot, bring out what goodies we had brought to share with Stuart, and reminisce into the wee hours of the morning, temporarily forgetting the work awaiting at sun-up. The stories became ever bigger and better as our resounding laughter made the candle flames flicker, dancing happy shadows across the walls of that often lonely, powerless shanty.

∞

It was during those adventures to Mathinna and Upper Esk that I got to know an old guy in Mathinna. A very colourful character, if I recall correctly, his name was Cyril, but he was always known as Screwy. He was even called that to his face, with no offence taken.

Following the night masquerades spotlighting, we'd leave Stuart's and head back to Mathinna, crossing the South Esk River to climb our way back over the Mathinna Plains to Ringarooma. On the outskirts of Mathinna, set amongst a couple of rusty, wrecked car bodies, were a couple of old shacks, one more dilapidated than the other. At least there was a power line linked to each of them. In the one closer to town lived Screwy.

We'd often be careening past at about 10 or 11pm, when someone would say, "Let's call in and see Screwy." If Mike was driving he would quickly pull the handbrake on, causing the car to spin dangerously out of control, at least that's what it felt like. In an instant, we'd be back facing the way we'd come, sitting in a cloud of dust. Shrieks of fear could be heard faintly over the rush of gravel and the roar of the engine. Everything was completely under control...

Mike often did those manoeuvres racing into the yard at his family's home in his FJ Holden. The back of the car would slide in one direction, then he'd blithely flick the steering wheel and the back end would swish the other way, narrowly missing the garage on one side and the house on the other. The car would shudder and stabilize when it hit the concrete, whizzing in around the clothesline at ninety degrees before coming to a sudden and safe stop a few feet from the back door.

Phew! Lucky no one was ever racing out of the back door at that moment. I guess they all knew what to expect when they heard the familiar sound of the old hotted-up FJ tearing up the drive, so they'd stay safely behind the door until he was stationary outside their shield.

Young and stupid you might say, our blood rushed through our veins at a furious rate of knots, pumping us with enough adrenalin to keep us awake for forty-eight hours straight. We'd drive right up to Screwy's door, jump out and rattle on his window, waiting for, "Who's there, who's there!?"

"It's Mike, Screwy."

A light would go on and we'd hear mumbling coming from inside, which was only one narrow split paling away from us. It must have been freezing at night for poor old Screwy. Somehow he survived with blankets from the Salvos, and probably slept close to his dogs to keep warm. If you went there through the day, the door would be open and there'd be a few dogs and half a dozen chooks walking in and out of his little shanty. At night, he'd warily open the door until he recognized one of us, then he'd give us a big welcome and stoke the fire up, jovial as ever. He'd swing an old kettle over the fire to get it cranking for a cuppa.

He was full of yarns, old Screwy. He reckoned he and his mum sang in the Sydney Opera House and he held the top note of Danny Boy for five minutes. I think that was a bit far-fetched. Anyway, we'd get him singing and telling stories. He looked at me one of the first times I went there.

"Who's this?" he asked.

"Pete Robertson," I introduced myself.

"Robertson, Robertson," he went, then, "I know your father."

"How so?" I asked, disbelieving.

"He was up in Cairns during the war. With his brother," he said.

I was gobsmacked.

"They were medical blokes, good fellas, good fellas," he went on. I laughed, still a bit hesitant to acknowledge that simply from my face he could tell me that.

"What did you do?" I queried.

"Me, I commandeered the South Seas," he boasted, "I was in charge of the fleet of ships patrolling the Pacific." It was hard to believe. This old lunatic in charge of the Australian Navy fleets during the Second World War? But then again, he seemed to know more about my dad and uncle than I'd have given him credit for.

I went home and told Dad about this old guy who was a kangaroo or two short in the top paddock, saying that he knew him from Cairns during the war. Dad racked his brain, but couldn't for the life of him recall a Cyril Cox. Some time later, Dad and Mum were holidaying down the East Coast. On their way home through Fingal, Dad suggested on a whim to go and meet this old Screwy Cox. He drove into the outskirts of Mathinna and immediately spotted his old house by my description. Doors were wide open. The chooks and dogs were home, but Screwy was nowhere in sight. The neighbour was in his yard, so Dad yelled out and asked did he know where Screwy was.

"Oh, he went up the street a while ago, he should be back soon if you want to wait." This neighbour, who lived there with his wife and young family, had befriended Screwy and looked out for him a bit. The interesting fact is this same bloke worked with Rob, my brother, when Rob did his building apprenticeship in Devonport. He was one of the builders when the whole crew from their work built a house from scratch to lock up in a weekend for one of their mates who'd lost his house in a fire. Guess where that house is? It's neighbouring our house where we live at Forth now! I find that fascinating!

Rob pointed the house out to us when he first visited us here. We call it Madge's old place. Madge lived there for about eight years after retiring, and now her nephew lives there with his partner. Madge was an old neighbour of my parents when they lived at Roland on their first small farm. Amazing. My mum lived here, in a little cottage on our place, for the last ten years of her life, and she and Madge would catch up and reminisce about old times quite often. There certainly are some odd twists and connections in life when you want to take time to explore.

Anyway, Mum and Dad couldn't wait for Screwy, but on the way back to Fingal decided to drive up and back down the main street of Mathinna, having been there very infrequently, if at all, during their lifetime. Mathinna was an old gold mining town. The relics of the mine are still visible, but the mine shaft is too dangerous to access now. Lo and behold, who should they see sauntering down the street but old Screwy (they guessed it was him from my vivid description). Dad pulled the car up and hopped out, allowing Screwy to meet them.

Screwy held up his hand.

"Wait a minute, wait a minute," he said, "Robertson!"

He remembered Dad from the 1940s in Cairns. What an amazing memory! Maybe he was in charge of the Navy! My Dad vaguely remembered him as washer up for the cook at the military camp at Cairns, but what is real? In Screwy's mind he was in charge of the fleets of the Southern Seas, and he sang with his mum at Sydney Opera House. Incredible. And there's more!

One school holidays, there was a young boy staying with relatives at Mathinna. Screwy told us this story himself, and others at Mathinna know it's fair dinkum (true in other words!). Screwy said wherever that young boy was over those summer holidays there was a beautiful, grand golden eagle flying overhead. Eagles brought good luck in Screwy's books.

Screwy did some research, and found there was a 'Golden Eagle Lottery' based in Adelaide. So he bought a ticket, half in his name and half in the young boy's name. It was to be drawn a couple of months following the boy's return home, but Screwy began celebrating winning the lottery weeks in advance of the draw. He was shouting people drinks at the pub and telling them what he was going to do with the money. The locals thought he was troppo and didn't believe a word of his ramblings, yet were willing and eager enough to accept the free celebratory beers.

Well blow me down—he won alright! $250,000, so $125,000 to the young boy in Adelaide and $125,000 for Screwy. He said the golden eagle came swooping back the day he won and tipped his wing to him. He hadn't seen the eagle since the young boy had gone! Unbelievable, and yet Screwy believed it, felt it and lived it weeks before it was drawn. So in reality, where there is no time and space—only now, Screwy had won six weeks before. He truly lived and believed he had won, and he did. As simple as that! And yet not so simple, because we let our minds get in the way, and before we know it the doubts are more real than the thing we believe we'll get or what we desire.

Russell received a brand new GT Falcon, and Screwy bought the pub, with grandiose ideas of what to do with it. He got Russell to run it for him and I think paid him most of the proceeds. Screwy lived at the pub for a while, in the laundry on a mattress I was told, but it wasn't long and he was happily back in his old rundown shack with his dogs and chooks. He ended his days as a resident in the nursing home at St Mary's.

There certainly aren't many of those old characters left around the place. He may have been screwy (had a few loose screws), but his life was most likely happier than most millionaires. His neurology certainly couldn't handle money, but he can teach us a thing or two. You will get what you truly believe, whether it's good or bad, so you may as well believe you are going to have, or are having, a brilliant life! Also, we probably do need to work on our mindset and values to *retain* what we want.

· CHAPTER 10 ·

Mates

After finishing school, I decided to have a year working before I went to university, mainly because I didn't really know what I wanted to do. At first, I did shift work as a freezer tunnel operator at Edgell's vegetable processing plant in Devonport. I had to sit for eight hours each day, watching processed veggies spill evenly onto a conveyor belt where they were transported through a tunnel to be snap frozen. It sure taught me that I wanted, or rather needed, to keep learning in order to do work I liked.

We weren't supposed to read or take our attention off the belt for one second. During breaks, when the women on the sorting belts went for lunch or smoko, I would turn the tunnel belts off for the twenty minutes for a reprieve from the constant vibration and escape into *Lord of the Rings*. I ended up reading all three books while working there, although it was almost the cause of my demise. After one such meal break, I became so engrossed in Frodo's adventures I was unaware the women had returned to work until I heard the 'splash, splash, sloosh' of sliced beans spilling over the platform where I worked.

In a panic, I quickly switched the belts on, but the beans were six inches thick, they would never freeze properly. I raked them out and pulled more onto the platform so they were about two inches deep on the belt. Surely they'll freeze now? But what if the supervisor comes now and sees all those washed beans? I'll be fired for sure. I grabbed the high-pressure hose used to wash the tunnel at night after production had finished, and after ten or so minutes managed to wash the last remaining evidence nicely out of sight and down the drain.

Phew, I was safe. The supervisor was known to be pretty strict. The next day, just in casual passing, he asked me, "How was the book?"

He must have known, I can't be sure, but that was all I needed not to read on the job ever again. I must have been doing a good enough job not to be retrenched. I respected him a lot more than most of the other workers there did. They thought he was harsh. I knew better.

I stuck it out for five months, probably the longest five months of my life. I think the season came to an end, so the decision was made for me to move on. I worked for Tim and Mary for a while, then like most young blokes, Mike and I were a bit restless and on the lookout for a bit of excitement, so we decided to go and have a look at what the rest of Australia had to offer.

We set out in our old EH station wagon, camping on a mattress in the back. We cooked out in the open on a gas cooker on the wagon's tailgate, and camped beside beautiful beaches all up the east coast of mainland Australia. Life couldn't be better. Although we called here and there for the odd job or two, employment seemed to be at an all-time low for casual seasonal workers. Travelling as far north as Cairns, we lapped up the beautiful hot weather that we experienced for only a few months a year in Tassie, if we were lucky.

While sunbaking after a dip in the pool at Cairns, stretched out on our towels as our lily-white skin turned nice shades of pink, suddenly we heard a bit of a stern mother's voice not far from us. We noticed a woman pick up her little infant, who looked as if he could only just walk. She marched over to the pool and threw him in. We looked on aghast, speechless at what we'd just seen! We could see the little bloke's arms and legs thrashing wildly near the bottom of the pool, then slowly he came closer to the surface.

Mike and I were holding our breath for the poor little mite. Eventually, after what seemed like an eternity, an older chap grabbed him and hauled him to the surface, then handed the gasping toddler back to his mum, saying, "Sorry, I couldn't see him there for a while."

I'll give you a while with your head under water and see if you like it! That was my first thought. As the mum marched off we heard her say, "So now you know what'll happen if you get too close to the pool!" Mike and I looked at each other in disbelief. We thought we could recommend this to schools on how to teach water safety! Incredible.

After being larrikins, enjoying ourselves as much as we could on our limited budget, we set off to Karumba near Normanton, at the bottom of the Gulf of Carpentaria. Oh, I forgot, something just popped into my head—we weren't misbehaving too much it seems, our parents could have been proud of us. We actually went to one of our little Sunday morning meetings at the home of an elderly lady, Mrs Styles! There was Mrs Styles, her daughter Marylin, Mike and myself. We sang a couple of hymns, prayed, and spoke a few of our thoughts of a spiritual nature of what had been important to us during the week.

When Dad arrived in Cairns in the 1940s, legs dangling from the back of an Army truck laden with fresh recruits from southern parts of Australia, they had driven past an attractive girl on a pushbike and Dad had wolf-whistled at her. So much for the shy young lad from Tasmania! On the next Sunday morning, Dad and Uncle Ron went to a little Sunday morning meeting in this same home. Dad must have gone extremely red when he recognized the girl sitting opposite him as the same one he'd wolf-whistled a couple of days before. They did have a crush on each other, but Dad's heart was set on that beautiful, petite girl from Beechmont, so it didn't eventuate into anything.

Now here I was at the same age, nineteen, sitting opposite that same sweet Marylin we used to tease Dad about. Perhaps she had meant it with Dad all those years ago, as she was still unmarried. A couple of years later I was to see my own soulmate or true love for the first time, riding a pushbike home from school as I drove past as a passenger in a truck. I still remember that beautiful long hair blowing in the wind, falling gracefully over a red overcoat I'll never forget.

There was a lot still to transpire in my life before that

unforgettable moment. Mike and I continued on our merry way down to Cloncurry, out to Mt Isa, then Alice Springs. No work anywhere meant we had to keep travelling, our holiday slush fund wasn't going to last forever. We travelled the very corrugated road to Ayres Rock, as it was known then. Uluru. Our teeth chattered all the way, and well after we arrived our bodies were still jittering from the vibrations. We slept the night in the back of our van and watched the glorious sunrise on to the great rock the next morning, still snuggled up in our sleeping bags, with the tailgate open to the sounds of nature as we woke up to another splendid, sunny day.

We drove to the start of the climb. The path looked nice and smooth, so we decided to run up in bare feet. Halfway up there was a rope to help pull ourselves up a rather exposed piece of the rock. Perhaps we'd been a bit foolhardy thinking it was a pushover. We reached the windblown pinnacle, marked clearly with a manmade cairn. The view of the Olgas was stunning. Quickly, we asked someone to snap a picture of us together at the top to prove we'd been there, before commencing the same path in the downward direction.

Gravity pushing us down proved too much for the balls of our feet. The friction of the grey/red granite caused bulging blisters to form before we were even halfway down. Both limping awkwardly, we made it back to the car and set off for Coober Pedy, hoping to find good facilities to wash off all the travel dust and pop our blisters to relieve the pressure on the raw balls of our feet.

Arriving after dark, we bought tokens for the shower, stripped off, and lathered up under the beautiful warm water. Click. The water stopped! You're joking. We both hopped out and washed as much of the suds off at the sink, where there was only cold water. We didn't realize that Cooper Pedy, being nearly all built in the ground, relied totally on rainwater and hence the restricted use.

We hightailed it out of there, disgusted with the town known for its amazing colours. Beautiful opals contrast greatly with the dry barrenness you see above ground. We eventually booked into a motel at Port Augusta to prepare ourselves for the long-awaited surgery of draining the painful blisters on our feet. Ayres Rock seemed a long time ago.

Our next port of call was Hamilton, Victoria, to visit Rosie's family. Rosie and Mike had kept a relationship going after Rosie's visit to Ringarooma with her brother, Geoff. It was a welcome reprieve to be nurtured and fed by a mother again, to enjoy the company of good friends, and a delight to see Mike and Rosie enjoying each other's company. We climbed through the Grampians for a day too, before finally heading home.

Ten weeks on the road and we were back in Tassie. Our bank accounts were skun bare, but all in all we'd had a great adventure. Not once did Mike and I argue or have a tense moment. We seemed to understand each other and got on exceptionally well.

· CHAPTER 11 ·

Ranger

I'd applied for a job as a trainee ranger with the National Parks and Wildlife Service (NPWS). As a family, we all loved nature and the bush, bushwalking was in our blood. Years previously we'd all tramped into Lake Pedder before it was flooded, to save a memory and a sample of that pure white sand of a truly unique piece of wilderness now destroyed by progress. I sometimes wonder what will be left of those absolutely special places for my grandchildren, although I am becoming increasingly optimistic as I watch the younger generation's desire for a better world. I can't remember what I wrote on my job application, but I must have made an impression because I was called for an interview.

There were three positions in the second intake of trainee rangers. I think they'd taken six in the first intake and wanted a few more to fill positions in other parks. Looking back, it was all a budget decision, replacing an adult wage with a trainee to do the equivalent. Am I cynical? Maybe. They promised a theoretical component including school time as well. It was a brilliant way to become a ranger, instead of going to university and doing a four-year degree, I could get training with hands on experience.

The interview was slightly nerve-wracking, as I had to sit across from four uniformed rangers, all male if I remember correctly. Emancipation was still in the process in NPWS. Women weren't considered as strong as men to do all the manual labour needed to clear and maintain tracks, build huts and boardwalks, let alone have the stamina for search and rescue in midwinter snowstorms!

A few weeks of anxious waiting followed, then yippee! I was accepted. One of three, out of hundreds of applicants. It's not until writing now that I realize the enormity of this achievement. I was just so excited to have the job of my dreams, to contribute, and to help others appreciate the wonders of nature.

My first placement was with the rangers who patrolled the hunting seasons—mutton bird, duck and deer. We often had very exciting chases around rookeries, along lonely roads with our lights off in the hope of intercepting poachers. During the deer season, we had a tip off that someone had been poaching deer up in the highland, amongst the lake country. We'd obtained a search warrant and were on our way to see if the informant was correct or not. Along one of the deserted gravel roads we happened upon a few young blokes relieving themselves beside their beaten-up old Falcon car.

"Likely poachers," the ranger muttered as we pulled up while they quickly finished peeing.

"What have you been up to?" asked the ranger. I was the observer, learning the tricks of the trade.

"Nothing, just out for a good weekend, doing a bit of camping."

We could smell the alcohol they'd been consuming, the reason they were now standing in a row on the side of the road whilst emptying their bursting bladders.

"Can we have a look in your boot please?" asked the ranger.

"Sure, we've been doing nothing to hide." The boot revealed more grog, some fishing gear and a couple of firearms. No dead game out of season.

"Ok, have a good weekend. Don't drink and drive too much, take care," and we were on our way. We eventually found the isolated house we were looking for. A long drive led us to a yard with a few sheds with half a dozen very lively dogs who didn't appreciate us being there. Lucky for us they were securely chained, by the look of them we'd likely be severely mauled if the chain snapped. A shifty looking character emerged from the house, and we could also see a woman and a couple of kids peeking out through a crack in the closed curtains. It was mid-afternoon, a pleasant enough day, not too cool for such an elevated spot. The ranger produced the search warrant and stated our business.

The man protested that he had nothing to hide, but it made no difference, a search was going to be made. He obligingly opened his sheds, then led us to the house. I felt sorry for the young couple, their privacy being invaded by complete strangers who virtually accused them of breaking the law. A quick scout through the house also revealed nothing.

"Thank you, and sorry for intruding," offered my superior, "just doing our job."

"Well, no luck there," he stated.

It seemed these guys only gained satisfaction from their work if they actually caught someone doing the wrong thing. The uniform gave us power, we commanded respect and obedience. I wasn't used to that sort of thing. I wondered if police were the same, and only felt their work worthwhile if they booked someone.

Mrs Robertson (my great-grandfather's wife) was a Wyatt. I'm pretty sure, according to our family tree, there was lineage to a convict who was brought out from England. I think the DNA of that ancestor is still running strong in our family, as I tend to find myself doing as much as I can outside the authorities having to be in the know. My kids all seem to have a strong dash of it streaming through their veins too. Unpaid fines, speeding, drink-driving, driving without a licence, giving a false name, and believe it or not, most of the time they avoided conviction.

There's that word convict(ion)! Imminent threat of jail, her freedom being taken from her, and being separated from her family was the only thing that halted one of our daughter's indignant hatred of authority enough to make her toe the line. All the kids seemed to be tarred with the same brush. Grada always blames my convict inheritance, but I won't start on the stories on her side!

Can you imagine being sentenced to transport to the infamous penal colony at Port Arthur, Tasmania, just for catching a rabbit to feed your starving family? Sure, it was on someone else's land, but a rabbit? It seems strange to me how we can change from a loving, family-oriented person, to one demanding, and even overpowering, when we don a uniform.

When I was nursing, that uniform allowed me to do exactly the same. We didn't do things against consent, but that uniform certainly helped gain consent. I knew what was best for my patient, and always did my best to try to think of myself in their position. I felt patients and co-workers, including the doctors, did hold me in high respect during my time on the wards. Even now my name is sometimes mentioned to my son-in-law, who is now working one of my old workplaces from fourteen years ago. I would have achieved this even without the uniform, I'm sure.

Anyway, failing to uncover criminal activities, we drove back via Interlaken, a place where two lakes only have the road dividing them (named after a place in Switzerland). We were heading from there down the range to the highway to Hobart. We'd knock off early that day! Or would we?

Going through Interlaken, we were flagged down by irate fishermen. People camp along the edge of the lakes and fish most of the day away, often storing their cleaned catch in a fly-proof airy safe hung in a tree next to their camp. Someone had driven through during late afternoon, raided their safes, then taken off. We, bearing the sign of authority, were the ones responsible to enforce the law. It wasn't really our department.

"Could you please inform the police then?"

Alas, the radio wasn't picking up signal. We were right in a dead spot.

"Can you describe the vehicle?" we asked.

"Yes, it was a beat-up old Falcon, grey colour." We looked at each other.

"I reckon we know who took your fish," the ranger offered, but we didn't have their plate number. He explained we'd met up with them earlier. Probably their lack of having caught any fish, or shot any game, gave them the idea when they spied all those fish hanging right beside the road. Their courage spurred on by their skins full of alcohol, their fish were an easy catch. Now they'd be able to brag to their mates and family of what they'd caught.

"What time was it?" we asked.

"Oh, around 3pm," quipped a young bloke, eager to be in the conversation. It was now 4pm. They would be nearly in Hobart by now, if that's the way they were headed.

"We'll see what we can do." The ranger took names and phone numbers, then we drove off quickly, encountering the changing road conditions as it wound its way with hairpin bends every 100 metres or so down to meet the highway at Tunbridge. We hadn't gone two kilometres when we noticed the tell-tale signs a vehicle had skidded off the road on one of the bends, holing their sump on a large rock on the side, evident by a large pool of dark oil.

"I suspect we might be in luck," the ranger stated in a matter-of-fact tone as we followed a dark trail leading down the dusty, narrow road. No engine would keep going for long with the oil drained. We had thought we'd see them hitching a ride, not expecting the surprise awaiting us around one particularly narrow sharp bend.

There, balancing precariously over the edge of a steep precipice, was the beaten-up old Falcon. One young bloke was lying on the ground beside the car, immediately we thought he was knocked unconscious or hurt. We jumped out, only to find he was fast asleep on the most comfortable rocks he could find. The other two were stretched out, one on the front seat of the car, one on the back, both also in a deep, drunken sleep. Any movement could have sent their car crashing over the edge. Luckily, we were back in radio range, so were able to reach the appropriate authorities.

The police in nearby Oatlands said they'd be up when they could, which may be an hour or two, depending when the other officer returned from another callout. They also organized a tow truck. We cautiously opened the boot, to discover a nice little cache of fish that appeared to have been hastily thrown in amongst their camping gear during their dare-devilish raid on the safes at Interlaken.

One after the other the three dejected young men emerged from their slumber, to see uniformed figures staring down at them. Their fun weekend had turned into their worst nightmare, which need not have happened if they'd limited their drinks. Oh well, you live and learn. These young fellas were learning the hard way. Their wrecked car and hefty fines for theft, let alone their sore heads the next day, would hopefully teach them a thing or two about what a good weekend was all about.

We arrived back at base well into the night, with me catching a few hours of sleep before I had to travel to Bagdad to help another guy doing research on the Tasmanian Devils. It was my job to catch them, take blood and attach ear tags before releasing them. They certainly do look ferocious when confronted with a human and only one cubic foot of space to move about in. Sometimes, when I returned in the morning I would find a cage bent totally out of recognition where a large devil had used his massive, vice-like jaws to fight his way to freedom. Once confined to a nice dark hessian bag they'd quickly quieten down though, and were quite friendly, nonaggressive little fellas.

It was always a joy to see them scuttle away through the bush upon release. I was amazed at the number of times I caught the same one in the same trap. Their little brains mustn't be good at remembering, or rather perhaps were more controlled by the scent of dead meat. Hopefully my short interludes in the dry Aussie bush of Chauncey Vale may have helped to keep our unique Tassie devils from extinction.

· CHAPTER 12 ·

Wilderness Adventures

My next stint in the NPWS was at Mt Field National Park. As trainees we were shifted around to gain maximum exposure to the different areas of a ranger's life. We travelled up past New Norfolk, the salmon ponds at Plenty, and Westerway, before we finally began to enter the wilderness of Tasmania's South West. An amazingly rugged landscape, it was made much more accessible to the public when the Gordon River power scheme dammed Lake Pedder. It is still a beautiful mass of mountain ranges, interspersed between button grass plains and impenetrable rainforest. A place you could easily lose yourself in.

While stationed at Mt Field, all the staff were engaged in search and rescue training exercises. One such course included spending two nights out in the wild on top of Mt Anne, which was covered with a thick layer of snow. We hiked up the mountain carrying tents, cooking gear, food, warm clothing and rescue gear. You would have thought we'd have welcomed the top, given all the weight we carried. Alas, there was only bare open space covered with huge drifts of freshly fallen snow. Beautiful, yes, but the gale force winds with a blizzard blowing made it impossible to pitch our tents. We were directed to make igloo type shelters, but without the roof. Blocks of frozen snow were cut from the pristine white landscape to form a protective wall around where we were to pitch our tents. The indentations we carved out would be filled by morning.

This was new to most of us, so the excitement of adventure

combined with the physical hard work helped keep us warm as toast in that bleak environment. The wind howled all night and the blizzard outside brought visibility down to about a metre in front of you. Venturing outside the confines of the flapping nylon of our tents was discouraged, as it would have been very easy to become disoriented and lost forever.

The next day we jumped over the edge of enormous snow drifts built up on the side of the mountain, setting off some minor avalanche activity. Oblivious to the danger of any major collapse of the wall of snow, which would have hurtled us to a cold, wet grave, we began burrowing into the soft surface like dogs after a bone. We went deep and fashioned out a beautiful snow cave, complete with sleeping shelves, a place to cook, and an area to light a small gas heater. We were snug as could be.

Occasionally we would hear a deep rumbling as big sheets of snow broke away and plummeted to the bottom of the cliff face hundreds of metres below. The wind was still roaring, like a monster seeking in every crevice for its prey, and yet inside our cosy, warm cave you could hear a pin drop. What an oasis to escape that persistent buffeting of the strong westerly wind known as the Roaring Forties.

I have been lucky so far, and have never had to use these survival measures. Hopefully no emergency situation will eventuate to test my no doubt rusty skills! At the time though, it was fun and broke the boredom of cleaning amenities and emptying rubbish bins - the glorious life of a ranger!

I once did a ten-day hike with my brother Rob, Joy (his wife) and a friend, through the Eastern Arthur Range and scaling Federation Peak to overlook the majesty of the whole area. Going up the face of Federation Peak we came to a spot where, when you peeked between your legs, all you could see was Lake Geeves—about 2000 feet below. Eek! Joy and I said we couldn't go any further as our legs had become jelly, but encouraged the others to keep going while we waited for them to return. We were only a few hundred metres from the pinnacle.

Just at that moment, a group of monks descended the peak. They could see our predicament and kindly offered us their climbing rope.

"Drop it off to us when you come back through Hobart," they smiled. We chatted for a while, sharing our adventures and plans. Our plan was that once we hit the Huon River at Craycroft Crossing, Rob would run back up to Lake Pedder and drive our car back down through Hobart, to where our track would end, where the Tahune Airwalk is now.

"Oh, we're finishing our walk at Lake Pedder," one of the monks said, "we can drive your car back around to Tahune if you'd like."

What a godsend! First a rope which made it possible for Joy and me to reach the top, then driving our car for us to where our ten-day hike was to finish. Unbelievable, it would take them way out of their way, probably adding three or four hours of extra driving.

"No worries," they smiled as we handed them our keys. There was no doubt in our minds that our car wouldn't be there waiting for us with the keys on the back tyre. It was a beautiful encounter, one that re-instils my belief in the goodness in humans whenever I think of it. And yes, the car was there!

We met another interesting character while we were on that hike. Carrying a pack of well over a hundred pounds, he'd been traipsing the wilderness all on his own for ten weeks. He must have been on a mission of self-discovery. Sometimes light aircraft would fly overhead, allowing tourists an eagle's eye view of our inspiring piece of the earth. The hiker would shake his fist at them as the drone of their engines shattered the peace the mountains shared as they loomed upward to the often-rainy skies above.

There were three trainee rangers stationed at Mt Field, two second years and myself. We shared a house with the storeman of the park. A little, rotund sort of bloke, he'd work his hours then head for the pub. We'd hear him come home at 10pm when the hotel hours ended, and were often woken in the middle of the night when a bottle hit the wooden floor. He'd be up and at work again at 8am. That was his life. We disappeared back home on our days off, but that chap stayed put. That was home for him. We didn't understand him, or rather didn't make the effort to.

We were all around twenty years old, and interested only in our own lives, so it seems now I'm looking back on things. I often wonder what happened to him. If he'd kept going the way he was, cirrhosis of the liver would surely have taken him at an early age. What had he been hiding from, not wanting to face up to what life had thrown his way?

At our current stage in life, Grada and I often help people to uncover their demons and work through their feelings, no longer needing to suppress those things too painful to look at. If only we could feel our feelings, our emotions, rather than pushing them under. Healing is in expression of the feeling. Yes, and how I wish I had learned this decades ago, before it almost destroyed my marriage.

The other couple of trainees were heavily into white water rafting. On a couple of occasions they persuaded me to join them on adrenaline-rushing adventures down rapids in rivers swollen with recent rains. One of the recruits in the same intake as me was a beautiful young girl, the daughter of Olegas Truchanas, a man from Lithuania who spent his life trying to persuade Tasmanians to preserve the beauty of their island. He was a WWII refugee who chose Australia as his home as it offered the most opportunity for freedom and encouragement for initiative. The other alternative was disappearing behind the iron curtain in communist USSR.

A prolific photographer, Olegas permanently imprinted the beauty of Tasmania's South West wilderness in the hearts of many. Tragically he drowned in January 1972, while on a canoe trip down the Gordon River Gorge. He was attempting to recapture a unique collection of photographs he'd lost in the devastating bushfires in February, 1967. A legendary figure in Tasmania, known for his wilderness exploration photography, Olegas Truchanas was a practical idealist who wished to preserve our pristine state in its natural beauty. I heard mutterings from other trainees that his daughter only got the position because of her father. Well, if she had his idealistic drive, who could better preserve our natural treasure for future generations?

His book, *The World of Olegas Truchanas*, showcasing lots of his amazing photography, was one of the books I packed a couple of years later to take to Europe. I'm sure it helped entice Grada to come to Tasmania, maybe even to marry me. She teases me that she fell in love with a wild Tasmanian bushranger, and reminds me often that what I mainly wore when I first arrived in Holland were my green NPWS trousers and jumper with their uniform khaki shirt! (In my defence, it was the warmest set of clothes I had after leaving the heat of Queensland to arrive in the freezing November winter in Europe.)

• CHAPTER 13 •

The Weir

After experiencing the thrill of white water rafting with my colleagues, I wanted more. I bought my own raft and trialled it a time or two on the calmer waters in a couple of the rivers near home. One weekend I was alone at home, as Mum and Dad were on holiday in Queensland. I'm not sure now whether Grandma was still alive or not, they could have been to visit her in the nursing home where she died, still quite embittered with life. In our church, there were what we call special meetings, where extra preachers fly in from interstate or overseas to give us an extra boost to help keep our faith alive. I'd invited Mike down to stay the weekend, planning a raft down the Forth River on Saturday, followed with special meetings at Devonport on Sunday.

There'd been quite a bit of rain, so the power stations were running, keeping the river flowing strongly. There wouldn't be any rapids due to it being brimful. No white water that day, but it would still be fun. We donned our life jackets and set in at the Paloona Bridge after borrowing my parents' car to get us there. It needed a drive every now and then was my excuse, but really it had a lot more grunt than mine. Impressions on your mate counted at age twenty.

The water quickly propelled us downstream. We hardly had to do anything other than lie back and watch the trees lining the riverbank whizz past. The weather was kind to us, sunny, although there was a bit of a chilly breeze. The water was freezing, rushing down from thawing snow in the mountains.

This was the life. Mike's sister and my cousin were following us down river by car, catching glimpses of us at times when the river came close to the road. Approaching closer to Forth, we could see them on the bank, waving to us. We steered our little craft closer to the bank, intending to finish our thirty-minute sail down river at that point, until I said excitedly, "Let's go over the weir!"

Years before, a weir had been built, traversing the river to allow a damming effect so water could be pumped out to supply the town of Devonport with water. The weir had proved dangerous for people trying to cross it by foot, a few people had even drowned. But we were just going to go over, and maybe continue down to the mouth of the river a couple of kilometres further downstream, with Turners Beach as our landing pad. We pushed cautiously out into the strong current which would take us gliding over the four-foot rapid at the middle of the weir.

Adrenaline rushed through our veins. Over we went, hoping to be rushed on further downstream. We landed in what seemed like a monstrous washing machine. The water racing over the weir resurfaced and churned back in under the fall, carrying our little craft back in under the cascading current to be turned over and over.

Lucky we had our life jackets on, I thought.

We resurfaced, spluttering, taken totally by surprise. Quickly, we clambered back into the raft, trusting we'd be swept away from that ugly backwash. In no time, we were again being churned like butter, not knowing which way was up or down.

At one stage I came up for air under the upturned raft. Catching my breath, the thought dashed through my mind, "They'll think I've disappeared," so grabbing the rope around the side of the craft I pulled myself up onto the bottom of our helpless boat.

Mike was clinging to the rope. I don't think he could swim.

"We were fools! What were we thinking?" I yelled out to him.

Again, the boat flipped, over and over. I tried kicking it away from the wall of concrete as we were swept in, time after time.

By now there were panic stations on both banks of the river. People were running up and back, not knowing what to do. Cars were pulling up. Even a police car arrived.

My hands were starting to go numb from the freezing water.

I seemed to be able to stop us being pulled back in under the fall, but I started losing my grip on the side of the raft. I curled one set of fingers firmly through the roll lock where the oar used to be. The oars were long since swept down the river and out to sea. I shouted to Mike to do the same, to cling with one hand or fingers through the ring, so when our hands froze solid we wouldn't lose our hold.

· CHAPTER 14 ·

Fools

I'm not sure how long it was before everything became blurred. A beautiful, warm sensation flowed through my body, everything was peaceful. Everything was as it was meant to be.

It felt amazing.

An incredible sense of peace.

Blissful.

I laid my head on the side of the raft.

The next thing I remember is shivering violently, not knowing what was happening. I was alone, in a hospital bed I guessed. Although I was under what felt like a dozen blankets, I was shaking like crazy.

My first thought was, "Where is Mike?"

It was terrifying, horrible. I can't describe it.

After what seemed like hours of drifting in and out of a sort of sleep, a nurse came in to check on me.

"Where's Mike?" I blurted.

"I don't know," and a shrug and was all I got. I watched her back disappear out the door.

"Oh shit! What's happened? Surely he's next door? What if he's thinking the same as me? Where is everyone?"

My thoughts kept whirring like I was in a nightmare. Perhaps it was all a dream. I tried not to think of the predicament we'd gotten ourselves into. What nuisances we must have been. Where was Mike?

Finally, someone came into my room. A doctor, by the look of the white coat.

"Where's Mike?" I pleaded again, "Where is he?"

The answer seemed to come from an eternity away, if there is such a place.

"It was too late for your friend, he is dead." He turned and left. That was that, I was all alone.

Surely not. No, there's been a mistake! Where was everyone then? Someone I could trust, a familiar face? There was no one. I had thawed out now, and still no one.

What if he really was dead? It was my idea to go over the weir. I'd suggested it. Oh hell, where was he?

Had I killed my best friend? If he had died, I remember my last words to him, or at least some of the last.

"We are fools." I'd called my mate a fool. The last words he heard me say. I was numb. I desperately wanted to cry but no tears came. Where was everyone? That feeling of being totally alone crushed in on me.

I wanted to scream. My terror wouldn't let me. I seemed to be tied down, unable to move.

∞

Footsteps, coming closer.

I think it was Colin, and maybe Tony, my cousin. Of course, everyone was here for special meetings. That's why Mike had come for the weekend.

"Where's Mike?" I pleaded.

They sat on my bed and slowly related the story to me. My hand clenching the row lock had saved me. Mike had also lost consciousness from that icy-cold water, hypothermia taking its toll, and had slipped off the side of the raft. A seasoned swimmer and lifesaver offered to go out and save us, so the police had tied a rope around his waist and he entered the river a long way up stream. That way he would be carried by the current to where we were stuck fast by the maelstrom. Apparently, before he reached the weir he beckoned to be pulled to safety. They threw ropes in at the same point, hoping we may be able to grab them and be pulled in.

It seems our rescuers were unaware that we knew nothing of what was happening. We were blissfully at peace. Everything was perfect, words can't describe it.

One of the ropes swirling around and around with the eddies became tangled around either Mike or my legs and we were dragged to safety. I still showed signs of life, only just apparently, so was the first to be loaded into a waiting ambulance and rushed away.

According to my cousin Janet, who watched on helplessly the whole time, when Mike was pulled onto the rocky bank he opened his eyes and looked her in the eye, a faint smile on his face. She told me later, and it was her way of acceptance.

"He was baptized in his death," she said.

Mike had 'made his choice to serve God' in a meeting when he was twelve, but never prayed or spoke in a meeting. He was seen as not having understood, and hence unbelieving, not saved. So for Gert (Janet's nickname) that was a great comfort, knowing he was baptized at his death. In the Christian belief, baptism by water signifies dying to self, then the coming up out of the water signifies being risen with Christ. To be honest, Mike didn't like a lot of the hypocrisy that goes on, even in the most enlightened churches.

During our talks together, Mike mentioned more than once that he wouldn't see twenty-one years. Here we were, both twenty, and he was dead. From his class at high school, out of twenty-four or so kids there were now only two left alive. Something uncanny was happening, as if a curse was put on that group at school. Mike had told of tales at school where his Uncle Irwin was a tech teacher. He was a German who lived in Berlin during the Second World War, aged fourteen when it ended. He witnessed things no young boy should have ever been allowed to see.

The kids at school soon knew his weaknesses and drove him to distraction every single day of his working life. So much so, that he was known to have thrown hammers and screwdrivers at students. Luckily no children were ever injured, and Irwin retained his position. At the end of class Irwin would loudly pronounce in his thick German accent, "Eh, eh, eh, pack up time!" This would be echoed back to him from multiple corners of the classroom, with varying degrees of accuracy when it came to the accent. His patience was tested to the limit, poor man. Maybe when he was fuming mad a curse escaped his lips a time or two? The statistics of twenty-two out of a class of twenty-four kids being dead by age twenty-one must be unheard of.

I was still in a deep state of shock, not only from almost dying myself, but I'd lost my best mate, my only good friend. You could say I'd as good as caused his death. That is what was coursing through my mind. Our youth had come to an abrupt end, over in a click of my fingers. Twenty years over, gone as quick as a flash. If I lived my expected seventy years it would be two and a half more clicks of my fingers.

What is life all about? Why? Why?

No answers came. Only guilt.

I'd caused Mike's death. I'd taken away Tim and Mary's eldest son, the family's fun-loving brother. How could I ever face them again?

Apparently, my Uncle Bob had said to Tony and Colin, "Don't let him blame himself for this." Did that mean others blamed me for it too? How could they stop me blaming myself, anyway?

Sunday, the next day, the special church meetings were a very sober, subdued congregation of people. I was allowed to go home. I had recovered with no ill effects from my hypothermic near-death state, which thinking back on the experience would be a very peaceful way to depart this scene, to where, I wasn't really sure anymore.

Surely a loving God wouldn't have allowed this to happen?

Joe and Ruth picked me up during the lunch break, between meetings. Mum and Dad were still in Queensland, organizing a premature end to their holiday to be home with me. I sat right at the back of the meeting, having gone in last to avoid the prying eyes and unwelcome condolences.

Eyes downcast, nothing much sank in, except I remember clearly what one preacher from South Australia said. He spoke about the two boys involved in an accident yesterday, with one boy, Mike, losing his life. He more or less said, I'm paraphrasing but can to this day remember it as clear as anything, that we shouldn't have been rafting down the river, enjoying ourselves, but rather should have been preparing ourselves for the Sunday meetings the following day.

In other words, we should have been reading, praying and meditating.

Another wave of guilt washed over me.

I heard later that Uncle Bob had taken that preacher out fishing in his boat on Saturday—about the same time that we were rafting down the river, the big fat hypocrite. I still feel angry when I think of his accusations.

• CHAPTER 15 •

The Slow Drive

The days blurred into each other.

I faced my second family with trepidation on the day of Mike's funeral. I don't recall any communication prior to that. Mum and Dad were home, but no words could console. It was a quiet, sad house at Larksfell, their home.

I travelled with Mum and Dad to Ringarooma that dreaded day, a two-and-a-half-hour drive. It was wet and dreary. Coming over the range called the Billycock, where you catch the first glimpse of that secluded rich farmland, we were met with multiple rainbows dancing over the hills. This was God's promise not to destroy the world by flood ever again.

Could this be an omen to a bright future? It certainly lifted my spirits as we pulled up to a tearful reunion with a very sad and shattered family. I was welcomed as a son and brother, one of the family. As we sobbed and clung to one another I felt no blame from anyone, although the wiggle of guilt bored deeper and deeper as I observed parents who'd lost their oldest son, brothers and sisters who had lost their laughter. The life of the party was no longer in their midst.

The funeral was held at Mike's uncle and aunt's property, the prestigious family home. The casket was open, and people filed past to pay their last respects. I went in mainly to make sure it was Mike. I hadn't seen him since I'd laid my head on the side of the raft and drifted off into oblivion. I hadn't seen him dead.

I looked down into the coffin to see my old friend. He wasn't there! Anna, his sister, was beside me.

"Hey Anna," I said, "Mike's not there. He's gone. It's only his shell."

The Mike I'd known wasn't that pale waxen form. The spirit had gone. Mike had gone. I bet he was observing everything that was going on. Anna hurried away, unable to grasp what I was getting at, perhaps thinking I had gone mad with grief. She wasn't the only one who was going to think that in the next few months.

I was one of the coffin bearers, so was in the car following the hearse which crept along at a snail's pace down Northview Lane. We all agreed it was the slowest Mike had ever travelled down that stretch of road. He had been a bit of a hooligan on the road.

I remembered the times we travelled to Launceston in his old FJ, with Johnny Cash's music blaring from the tape deck, and the squeal of tyres going around the bends on the sidling. It was always a contest to see if we could get there in under an hour. Normally an hour and twenty minutes would get you there if you stuck to the speed limit.

Once, Mike and I were in Launceston and needed to be in Latrobe to pick up Lisa, his girlfriend at the time, when she finished her shift at the hospital at 3pm. Well, knowing us, we left a bit late, but if the road was clear we'd make it. Mike was driving his parents' Kingswood at the time. We went via Exeter down the Frankford highway. Just as we were leaving the Tamar behind after heading west from Exeter, a clown in a later model Holden dared to overtake us. Needless to say, he didn't get very far ahead of us! We stuck to his tail all the way until almost Moriarty. He'd fishtail out of the corners with us close behind. At one stage I ducked involuntarily as the back of his car hit a temporary road works sign, sending it flying in our direction.

Just before Moriarty, close to Latrobe, he slowed right down in front of us. Was he conceding defeat?

Did he have to stop to change his pants?

We went sailing past, only to have him speed up beside us—flashing a card at us.

"Oh shit, he's a cop."

We pulled over. He came up to Mike's window and let out a string of very colourful expletives, then proceeded to write a ticket on quite a number of charges. When we limped into Latrobe, Lisa was waiting impatiently for us. We would have made it if he hadn't pulled us up. We laughed all the way to my place, still high on adrenaline. Mike didn't hear any more about that incident. I reckon the constable wouldn't have had his job after standing in court with both our statements showing what sort of example he'd set. We would have done it in forty-five minutes, we often said to each other with a laugh, as we remembered the way the cop had been driving.

Yes, Mike certainly had the slowest car trip ever as he was taken to the graveyard at Alberton, where other older members of the Jones family had been laid to rest. The skies cleared as we stood around the open grave. I remember nothing of what was said that day, but when I watched the shiny wooden box lower into the damp, cold hole in the ground, I became inconsolable.

It was horrible, and I couldn't get it out of my head that I had caused it. If only this, if only that, or if only I hadn't bought that blasted raft. The tears flowed for my lost friend. I'd actually become quite jealous of Mike's attention to other people. He was *my* friend. I realized he was friends with everyone, but he was really my *only* friend.

And now he was gone.

I must be meant to be alone.

· CHAPTER 16 ·

Love and Joy

Jack, the park ranger at Mt Field, couldn't have been more uncaring if he'd tried. He used to say, "Just get over it boy," when I was feeling lost and alone. I'd withdraw and prefer my own company. Looking back, he was probably trying to snap me out of my misery, but he seemed mighty cold and harsh to me at the time. Luckily, I was moved to Entally House, where my lodgings were a couple of rooms attached to the little church. There, after work, I was completely alone. The other blokes working there lived elsewhere and I was on my own in that grand estate, alone with the ghosts of the past, and dare I say of the very recent past.

From a small child, and all through my youth, I'd felt lonely, as if I didn't fit anywhere. That was until I'd found Mike. My life changed, I'd found a friend, one I'd become jealous of. I remember another young bloke had moved to Ringarooma and was working for Mike's family. He was our age and got on well with Mike. I let myself get dragged down with envious resentment often. Then eventually, after a lot of pestering, Mike had agreed to come for that fateful weekend, and I had killed him. I'd ruined that amazing friendship.

Was I destined to be lonely, alone, or was it something in me resonating messages to the universe, something within my unconscious self?

I was too miserable to explore those possibilities, rather romanticising my friendship with Mike as being like David and Jonathon's bond. King David from the Bible I mean, who had a blood oath with the son of Saul. Occasionally I'd get a visit from some young acquaintances from Launceston, or my cousin Janet. They were keeping an eye on me, I thought.

I remember watching *Jesus Christ Superstar* at the cinemas during that time, again feeding my guilt, watching that 'blasphemy.' That is what my conditioning led me to believe, about anything that wasn't a part of *The Way* I'd been brought up in.

During my vast alone time, something remarkable happened. I can't exactly remember when it started or what triggered it, all I know is I became filled with an amazing feeling of love and joy. Everyone, or you could say everything, I looked at gave me such a thrill. I was full to bursting with a love I'd never before experienced. This came from that place of extreme loneliness, and yet on the other side of it was bliss. I realised I would never have experienced it if Mike was still alive. I was in a place where I was extremely thankful for that experience of nearly dying and losing my best friend.

Everyone I encountered among my family and friends, I would try for all I was worth to explain how I felt and that I was grateful for Mike's death. I can explain it better now than I did then. No, I will never be grateful that Mick died, but I will always be thankful for the incredible sense of love and joy that flowed through me during my solitude that followed. There was an occasional one who seemed to understand what I was experiencing. Many, including my parents, thought and even said as much—that I'd finally cracked, the grief had sent me crazy.

It was so frustrating. How could I convince people of how I felt when they couldn't feel it? Eventually I gave up telling people. How could they know, when all they expected was to see me being sad?

Slowly those feelings of ecstasy evaporated, and with the monotony of work, cleaning toilets, keeping grounds and tracks clean and planting gardens, life returned to 'normal.' Years later I would experience this beautiful state again a few times, although to a lesser degree and for shorter intervals of time.

Grada has often asked me why I can't feel like that all the time, or a lot of the time anyway. I certainly wish I could. Looking back, the other times were also when I was totally alone. I still visited

Ringarooma often and shared in memories of Mike with his family, often with a mixture of laughter and tears. I was very close to them, his siblings were like brothers and sisters to me.

And yet they weren't, so the closeness developed into romantic feelings at times. Pam and I became friendly—more than brotherly/sisterly. Pam was two years older than Mike and worked at St Helens as a nurse at the hospital. I'd bought a road pushbike and decided to ride my lonely hours away. I had my first holiday from my job as a trainee ranger, and planned to ride from Ringarooma to Hobart, via the East Coast and back.

"I should be able to do it in the best part of my week off," I proclaimed.

I pedalled into St Helens after a long day, wearied by the mountain passes between Ringarooma and the East Coast. I had made that part of my journey in one day, then rested for a day or two. The couple who Pam boarded with were away, so we made the most of each other's company, and I almost lost my virginity! Luckily, Kevin and Lyn arrived home in the nick of time. My belief at that point was that I would have had to marry Pam if we'd had sex. I wasn't sure she was the right one!

The next day we went to a little meeting at Bicheno. I'm not sure whether almost having sex out of wedlock caused any guilt feeling during that time of worship or not. After the meeting, I set off on my bike towards the south and the others returned north to St Helens.

· CHAPTER 17 ·

Freedom

I was on my own. It sticks in my memory as a highlight in my life. That afternoon I saw a sheep in distress lying on its back, caught in the blackberries. I jumped the fence beside the road, and to my surprise found she was in the process of giving birth. She was in trouble. I helped her by extracting her from the blackberries, then assisted with the birth by gently pulling the lamb with the contractions. It was a thrill to see a live little lamb come slithering out. Riding away, I felt exhilarated to think maybe I'd saved two lives that day. Both the sheep and her lamb were on all fours and nuzzling one another when I left.

I reached Orford that night, pitched my tent and went to sleep with the sound of the waves lapping at the beach just ten metres away. What a wonderful feeling of freedom! I wondered if sex was as good as it was cracked up to be, compared to this feeling of being as free as a bird sailing on the wind?

Winding away from the sea the next morning, climbing upwards west of Orford, was hair-raising as log trucks raced towards me, cutting corners on their way to the mill at Triabunna. Tasmania was still being pillaged and plundered for its wood, a far cry from what Olegas Truchanas had envisioned. At least I was working for the NPWS, I kept telling myself, reassured that I was doing my bit to help preserve some nature for generations to come.

Hobart was my next port of call. I camped by the river at Sandy Bay before setting off north again along the Midlands Highway. Just out of Bridgewater, a familiar looking truck overtook me, then pulled up a bit further up the road. Out climbed Bill Watson. He limped down the road towards me, a big grin on his face.

"Thought I might see you somewhere!" he shouted. "Want a lift?"

Why not, it was kind of cheating, but spending time with Bill was a bonus. Years before he had carted things from Launceston down the North West Coast, a cut-throat sort of business as other transport drivers were out for their share of the market. They had licences that only allowed them to cart things in certain areas, but Bill didn't seem to take any notice of those restrictions. Sometimes, having been tipped off by other irate drivers guarding their territory, the transport police would pull him up and say, "How come we can never catch you out of your area?"

"I might look silly," was Bill's cheeky reply.

One day Bill's luck ran out, near Deloraine. He'd pulled up to check his load and was just hopping back into his truck when one of his opposition tore past in his truck, sideswiping Bill and his door, leaving him for dead on the road.

The same thing was to happen years later to someone much closer to me than Bill, bringing my whole world crashing down around my ears.

Anyway, after months in hospital, Bill hobbled out and got straight back into his truck and resumed his cartage business.

This was my lucky day. Bill was full of yarns (stories), he was a laugh a minute. Just what I needed to break the monotony of the busy highway. A few kilometres further up the road Bill pulled up for a woman who had her thumb up in the air, asking for a driver to stop and give her a ride.

"Shove over here in the middle mate," he said to me as she clambered into the cab. Bill and I looked at one another. I don't think either of us had witnessed a specimen of the opposite sex quite like this one before. She was pretty rough around the edges, to say the least. When she opened her mouth she confirmed our suspicions of her character. She was as uncouth as any person, including men. I think Bill was having second thoughts about always helping someone in a worse spot than himself.

We reached Oatlands nearly an hour later, with our ears ringing from words not found in the English dictionary. Bill pulled up outside the hotel.

"Anyone for a drink?" he asked.

"Oh yes $&#*ing please!" replied our passenger, leaping out of the cab.

"Quick! Shut the door!" Bill hissed as he slammed the old truck into first gear and took off up the road.

"That was a near miss, boy!" he said, grinning from ear to ear. He called everyone of the male species 'boy.' We made good time heading northwards. I'd have to get off at Conara junction and head towards Fingal. I may even make Ringarooma today, I thought.

Just approaching the small town of Ross, a police car overtook us with lights flashing, wanting us to pull over.

"I'll be damned," old Bill cursed under his breath as he crunched the gears to slow the old truck to a stop.

"Sorry to bother you, sir," Bill looked around at me, asking where the 'sir' was.

"We were told you picked up a lady just north of Hobart."

"No, that wasn't me," Bill said, "I didn't pick up any lady."

"We're sure you did sir, could you tell us where you last saw her?"

"Well, I picked up something, but I sure wouldn't call her a lady!" Bill chuckled. He relayed the story of what had happened. The police jumped in their car, did a U-turn and raced off back in the opposite direction.

"We had a lucky escape there, boy!" Bill laughed as we continued on towards Conara. "Hey, I can take you to Fingal if you like boy, there's someone there I want to catch up with."

"It's a bit out of your way!" I protested.

"No, she's fine boy, I'm in no hurry."

It would take him at least an extra hour to go to Fingal and back to the highway. That was Bill, he'd go right out of his way for anyone. Well, maybe not everyone, if they weren't a lady!

Once when he was going from Launceston to Burnie, he offered a guy a lift. As soon as the man got into the cab, he placed a revolver beside him on the seat, saying, "Take me straight to the Burnie wharf." If they met any police he'd quickly lift a newspaper up in front of him as if he was reading. Bill lent down to reach under his seat, hauled out a huge wrench and put it on the seat beside him as he kept driving. I'm not sure what Bill was going to do with his big wrench against a gun, but nothing seemed to faze him.

He did as the chap said, and went straight to the wharf area when he got to Burnie.

Hopping out of the cab, the man warned Bill not to go anywhere near the police.

"Oh, don't worry about that, boy," Bill drawled, "I'm in enough strife with them myself!" he laughed.

As soon as Bill left the wharf, he went straight to the police station and told them what had transpired. He was asked to describe the man.

"Just wait here for a moment," the clerk spoke curtly, leaving Bill no option. Half a minute later the clerk was back.

"Come through this way please," he ushered Bill into a room with an internal window that looked into another room.

"Is this the man?" he asked as Bill ducked down below the window.

"Don't worry," the clerk reassured, "one-way glass."

"My, you boys are good." Bill beamed as he sauntered back to the front desk.

Bill knew people everywhere and they'd welcome him in for a cuppa and a chin wag, which is exactly what he did that day in Fingal, making it an excuse so he could take me and my bike a bit closer to Ringarooma. A great bloke, but probably a bit of a nightmare for his wife, who mostly didn't have a clue where he was or when to expect him home.

He helped me down with my bike, then turned and limped up the path to an already opened door. Here he'd enjoy a cuppa and another good yarn, adding a few flourishes to the adventures he'd already had today. An extra one-and-a-half hours added to his day meant nothing.

"You only live once boy, make the most of it!" Relationships were certainly a big part of Bill's life.

I cycled through Mathinna, stopping to say good day to Screwy, then up over the plains to Ringarooma. What a day! Pam was home on days off. We both knew it wasn't the real thing, so after chatting into the night, agreed to be just friends, or like brother and sister again.

· CHAPTER 18 ·

Archaeology

My next work assignment was to experience some of the early history of Tasmania, joining a couple of archaeological expeditions. That would certainly be different! The first was at Bowen's landing on the Derwent River, where the first British settlement in Tasmania (then called Van Diemen's Land) occurred in September 1803. Forty-nine settlers made up of NSW Corp personnel, administration, free settlers and convicts, were under the leadership of twenty-three-year-old Lt Bowen of the Royal Navy, Devon. Bowen settled at Risdon Cove, just north of what was to become Hobart.

I camped onsite in my tent, cooking my meals either over a campfire or on a gas cooker in my two-man tent. That was the life! I was included as part of the team at the dig, carefully trowelling away dirt, centimetre by centimetre, or brushing dirt off the bricks which once were the foundation of the original buildings. The work was quite boring, interspersed with the occasional thrill of discovering something of real worth. A coin, a handmade nail, a key. Then the excitement would wane into boredom again, until the next find!

This was through the summer months, so many pleasant evenings were spent around the campfire with the other volunteers. I think archaeology relies mainly on volunteer labour, their reward being the excitement of uncovering history. I had my wage as a trainee ranger, which wasn't a lot as we were meant to be getting a theoretical education as well. Until that point, there had been no sign of any learning materials.

Every few months there was a training day where all the trainees come together. We discovered many of us were disgruntled at the lack of course material that had been promised almost eighteen months prior. Already one of the first group had resigned. The other trainees had heard of my disastrous rafting mishap, and their friendly commiserations were somewhat healing. The comradery of the group was warming to my soul, but they couldn't really understand what I'd been through. With that thought, I'd isolate myself from them, not letting them in.

In February I'd be twenty-one. Usually people make a big fuss about 'coming of age,' but I wanted nothing of the sort, and told everyone I'd be leaving the state. My next placement was to assist on a dig organised by a group from the University of Canberra. It happened to be excavating an Aboriginal midden near the Arthur River, way up on the north part of the rough west coast. On my 21st birthday I flew from Hobart to Smithton in a small twelve-seater plane, then the chap in charge of the expedition picked me up and we drove south, towards the Arthur River.

The camp was in the lea of the dunes, beside a small creek with brackish water in that untamed part of Tasmania. So, however briefly, I had actually left the land of Tasmania on my birthday, as I said I would. None of my family or friends really knew where I was, only vaguely, and I found it somehow satisfying that my 'coming of age' was minus all the fanfare.

Again, I was alone in my tent, whilst sharing a campfire with idealistic young university students from Canberra. It was a bit of a rude shock for some of them, as they were used to city life. We discovered eels in the creek, so I devised a trap from some of the gear they had brought for the excavations. There were sieves to sift the sand of the midden. With permission to wreck one, I made a funnel-type eel trap which we put a squashed-up sausage in, then left it down a dark pool.

After an hour of patiently waiting we'd managed to catch a couple of the slithering snake-like creatures. I was somewhat of a hero, but then I had to kill, skin and gut them. Not having done that before, I found it a bit daunting, but I couldn't be seen as a fraud. It all went reasonably well, even if I say so myself.

We cut the eel into pieces and skewered them on sticks to roast over the flames. Most of us had a taste of freshly roasted eel for the first time in our lives. Maybe not the finest cuisine for a 21st birthday party, but I'm sure it was an unforgettable time for all involved. Only I was aware that it was my birthday.

My time at the Arthur River decided for me that archaeology wasn't on my career wish list. The midden was mapped out into ten centimetre squares. Each square was carefully scooped into a plastic bag to the depth of five centimetres. Then the next layer the same. The bags were then taken back to camp, tipped into sieves where the sand was sifted out, leaving pieces of shells and rock. These were tipped back into the bag that had been labelled with the exact grid reference for where it had been in the midden. It was far too tedious and boring for this adventurous Tasmanian bushranger.

If anything, the experience triggered an urge for adventure. Given that the course material was still just in the wind, and a couple more trainees had resigned due to the fact that we were just being used as cheap labour, I too had had enough. I resigned, much to my parents' disappointment.

Mum once said we were all disappointments, because we didn't stick it out in what we had started. The twins started university and dropped out after a year, but Bernard did actually finish his technician course with Telecom, so I'm not sure why Mum felt disappointed with him. I know Rob almost didn't finish his building apprenticeship, I think they had to use threats to keep him at it. Joe wanted to farm after his father, even with his good academic brain, and Marg dropped out of nursing. I'm not sure what Mum would have chosen for us all, but we certainly knew what we didn't want to do!

• CHAPTER 19 •

The Passport Office

I decided I'd go and work the cane season for George at Koumala, near Mackay in Queensland. I drove to Queensland in my trusty little red Mini, stopping at a few places on the way, always on the lookout for another close friend, even a soul mate. There were a few attractive girls I may have upset, as I'd feel an attraction but then know they weren't the right one. Rather than try to persevere and make it work, I felt it was best to keep moving.

The cane season went from June to mid-November. I lived in a caravan on the cane farm and looked after myself. I would awaken at the crack of dawn, often to a brisk, cool start to the day. By 8am I was down to singlet and shorts.

I needed my truck licence, so George drove me in the truck to the Sarina Police Station, chewing a piece of tobacco in his toothless mouth all the way, saying, "She'll be hunky dory mate, you'll get it no worries." He must have known the policeman, probably his drinking buddy at the Koumala Pub, because he clambered in beside George and said, "Drive up the road to that old shed." It was about 500 metres away.

"Now turn around and drive back to the station."

That was it. I had my truck licence!

George drove the harvester and I was one of the truck drivers carrying the rail trolleys to and from the siding. I'd pull up beside the harvester and the cane would be cut into ten-inch pieces that were spat out into a cage on railway wheels. The old harvester often had mechanical problems! I'd hear George cursing under his breath as he removed already cut cane to get to where the problem was while I waited patiently, sweating my time away in the overheated cab. No movement made it almost unbearable in there at times, at least when I was travelling it created a bit of an airflow to evaporate the sweat and cool me off a fraction.

More than once I'd be daydreaming when suddenly I'd see a ten-foot carpet snake curled up in the top of the cane—right beside my open window. It was times like that I wished I had spare underdaks in the truck! All the snakes in Tasmania are poisonous, but the old carpet snake isn't. All the same, they scare the wits out of you when they are that close.

I made some good friends while working there. Usually I'd have the weekends free, and often spent them either with the Abels or up in Mackay. I got on especially well with Ken and Judy, a young couple with three adorable young kids. Colin and Naomi (Ken's brother) lived close by and they had four adopted children, also good fun to be around. They also had a pool, so many hours were happily whiled away enjoying their playful company. Towards the end of the season I was a bit undecided what I'd do. I had thought I'd go back to Tasmania and relieve my brother from milking his cows while he and his family went to the yearly Christian convention.

During my time in amongst the cane, I'd spent hours reading my bible and pondering over what was written. One weekend I drove my little Mini almost to the top of a mountain overlooking the district. It was a rough four-wheel drive track and I'd been up there before with Ken and Judy in their four-wheel drive. I got further in my Mini than we had that previous time, picking my way around protruding rocks. Eventually I had to walk the last few hundred metres.

Sitting alone on top of that mountain, I felt that same overwhelming love and peace I'd experienced after Mike's death. I believed it was God's spirit at that time, since I'd been giving a lot of attention to the scriptures. It felt amazing, whatever it was. An overwhelming love enveloped me from somewhere.

During that time of indecision, an invitation arrived to join my brother Winston, and his fiancé Krijn, for their wedding on the 23rd of November in Holland. I chatted with Ken and Judy about it, and Judy, full of enthusiasm said, "Why don't you go?"

"I was thinking of going back to Tassie to help Joe milk," I said, "and it'll take ages to organise my passport and ticket if I do want to go."

"Well, if you can get your passport and everything organised in four weeks, you'll be meant to go," stated Judy resolutely. "Go on and ring the passport office now."

Ring, ring, ring, ring.

"Hello, how can I help you?"

"Oh yes, how long does it take to organise my passport?" I asked tentatively.

"Six weeks."

"Are you sure, what if I came to the office?" I spouted hastily, as if to quicken the process.

"No, six weeks, sorry."

I must admit I did feel slightly despondent when I got off the phone. A seed had already been sown by Judy.

"I'll be going to Tassie," I stated triumphantly, almost to hide my disappointment, "it takes six weeks."

"Don't let that stop you," Judy rebounded, "ring the Townsville office, surely they could do it quicker than that."

I rang again.

"Hello, how can I help you?"

I asked the same question. The answer—three weeks.

"See, I told you, you were meant to go!" squealed Judy, bouncing up and down.

Three weeks, it would be touch and go. I'd need to fly in three and a half weeks. I set off to Townsville, a four-hour car trip, leaving at 6am so I could get back the same day. The clerk at the passport office gave me the forms to fill out—no one had told me I needed the signatures of two people who'd known me for more than two years! I was from Tasmania for goodness sake. There's no bending the rules in some of those bureaucratic offices.

Hey, wait a minute, "I might be in luck," I thought. An old girlfriend of Winston's was married now and lived in Townsville.

What was her name? I scratched my brain until it nearly bled, I reckon. Then I remembered, White. Janine White, but what was her hubby's name? I asked for a phone book and scanned the Whites. Something and J. Ah, there it was, M for Malcolm. My memory was proving itself. I'd only met Malcolm once or twice in Sydney when I stayed with Winston and James, back when James was studying at Hawkesbury College to become some sort of scientist! Something to do with milk and cheese-making, I think.

I had their address!

Knock, knock.

Janine opened the door with a hearty welcome. She was a mum now and home with her child, while Malcolm was away in Brisbane for work. Oh no, I needed two signatories. I explained my situation and about wanting to go to Winston's wedding. They'd also received an invite, but couldn't go. Then Janine remembered there was a guy visiting from Victoria by the name of Hanna, he was with the Airforce.

"Graham Hanna?" I asked, hoping beyond hope.

"Yes, that's him," Janine said, "do you know him?"

"Yes!" I exclaimed, "in our little meeting back at Ulverstone in Tassie we meet with Alan and Joan, and Joan is Graham's sister! He has been over in Tasmania quite a few times, I know him well." One down, one to go. Off I went to the Airforce base. There, after much questioning on their part and explaining on mine, they directed me to his address. He was home and signed the form for me.

Yippee! Back to the passport office. They were quite surprised, I think.

"Ok, where can we send it once it returns to us?" the clerk enquired, "it'll take three weeks."

"Oh, I'll come and pick it up in person," I replied, "I don't want it getting held up in the post."

He looked at me quizzically and asked, "What, you're going to drive all this way up and back just to pick up your passport?"

"Yep," and I explained why I wanted it, when the wedding was and when I needed to fly.

"Just a minute," he said as he disappeared through the door to a back office. After a few minutes he re-emerged.

"Come back at 3 o'clock and we'll have it ready for you."

"What?!" I blurted disbelievingly.

"Yes, you heard right, come back at 3 o'clock."

I turned and skipped out. If that wasn't confirmation that I was meant to go to Europe, what was? I rang Judy, all excited. She too was full of excitement. I could just see her jumping up and down full of enthusiasm for me. I can't thank her enough for being the catalyst to get me to Europe. Yes, I think I've already mentioned the girl on a bike in a beautiful red coat with her glossy hair flying in the wind!

· CHAPTER 20 ·

Hallo Grada!

I could just say the rest is history and leave it at that, but that's only half the story! The trip to Holland wasn't all beer and skittles, often casting some doubts back into that unbelieving brain of mine as to whether it was meant to be.

At that time Australia was often crippled by strikes, so my international flight out of Sydney was delayed by six hours. That meant I missed my connecting flight in Singapore, so instead of flying direct to Amsterdam I was to fly via London, then to Schiphol Airport in Holland. Oh well, there was still time enough.

Getting closer to England, we were told that London, or rather Heathrow, was fog-bound, so we were diverted to Gatwick airport— out in the country somewhere as far as I knew. I didn't have a clue, it was my first trip overseas. Everything was exciting, a new adventure. We landed at Gatwick, then boarded a bus to Heathrow, which was still covered with a thick, misty cloud. It was chaos, but somehow, although I don't remember much about it, I organised a flight to Holland. I think I must have blotted it out of my memory!

Arriving in Holland at Schiphol Airport, late evening towards the end of November, was quite a shock to my system after leaving sunny, hot Queensland! I was in a short-sleeve shirt with a thin pullover, so when I stepped outside after changing a few of my Aussie dollars, a warm taxi looked rather inviting, far preferable to spending any more time looking for buses or trains. I approached the taxi rank.

"Where to?" the driver managed.

"To Uitgeest," I tried to say, pronouncing it as, "Wheatgeesed."
"Where?"

I tried another couple of times, then pulled out paper and pen and scrawled the address out for the driver.

"Ohhh, Uitgeest!" he exclaimed, pronounced, "Outgaced," with a guttural "g." He spoke on the radio in a language that was all gobbledegook to me! I couldn't understand one word. I had only lived in Australia and spoken and heard English, except for a bit of French in high school, for which I received a second-rate pass for answering most of the exam questions with, "je ne sais pas," (I do not know). Incredible that I remember how to write even that in French.

Twenty to thirty minutes later, I and my luggage were deposited outside the door of what looked like a shop. It was freezing cold, so I very much hoped I had the correct address. This was supposed to be the home of my brother's fiancé, where he was also living. I knocked, knocked, and knocked harder. I could see into the house a little, and saw people through a couple of doors further in the house. Eventually, Krijn came to the door. Initially they'd thought someone was just wanting lollies from the shop (it was a lolly shop, snoop winked). Then Krijn said, "Oh, maybe it's one of Winston's family," and came to investigate.

Winston was out having tea with his boss's family in another part of town. They rang him and he came home, interrupting his visit. Winston had worked the cane season the previous year for George, so we had a good old catch up on news from Queensland.

Two years previously, Winston had travelled through Europe with some other Australians and visited one of our Christian conventions in Switzerland, where he met Krijn, who was on holiday. He'd thought she was Swiss initially, but luckily for us Aussies most European people can speak English. He spent the following year writing to Krijn. She wrote in Dutch, he in English, and with his trusty little Dutch to English dictionary he'd decipher her letters, often taking a few hours. A love was kindled, and now here he was, after spending a year here with her so they could get to know each other, they were getting married.

After a good chinwag I crashed, totally exhausted after about thirty-six hours of travelling. I was totally 'kaput' (a new word I had just learned, meaning broken or had it!). I thought I'd only just fallen asleep in the tiny 300-year-old attic bedroom, when I was being shaken awake.

"Do you want to come with me today?" Winston asked.

He was about to leave for work. He drove a truck, collecting old bread from bakeries all over Holland. These were put through a hammer mill, then dried into breadcrumbs to be delivered again throughout the country for pet food or fast food ingredients. The occasional unlucky mouse would sometimes unwittingly ride the loaf into the mill to become crumbs as well. A little added protein on your fish fingers or croquette wouldn't hurt!

I stretched and yawned, thinking it would be much easier to stay in bed, but then I remembered I was in another country! Everything was new. Excited for adventure, I jumped up and quickly donned my warmest gear. Winston offered me a thick parka jacket. I looked at him quizzically.

"You might need this," was all he said.

It was pitch dark outside. There was a thick layer of ice obscuring our view through the windscreen of his car.

"Do you want me to grab a bit of water?" I asked.

He laughed, and began tediously scraping the ice from the glass! The water would have frozen immediately, making the problem ten times worse. This wasn't Tasmania, apparently. We had to repeat the process for the truck before setting off on his rounds, the truck having been loaded the previous evening, ready for an early start. It was still dark, and remained that way for the first few hours of our journey. Eventually we witnessed the sun rising on an amazingly beautiful, frosty landscape.

Everything was so neat and tidy. Even beside the train lines little garden plots lay dormant, covered with straw for the winter months, waiting patiently for the spring warmth when they'd burst forth to produce plenty of food to feed a family in the adjacent village.

I was soaking in the new vistas all day long. There were often long silences. Us Robertsons could be like that, maybe from cellular memory from convict days in solitary confinement. Idle chatter seemed to be like wasting breath for us. Perhaps it came from the saying 'Children should be seen and not heard!' Especially at the table. Mealtimes at home were often quiet, everyone concentrating on the meal before them. We were taught early in life we had to eat everything on our plate, whether we liked it or not, as it was good for us. If we didn't, it'd be on our plates again at the next meal.

That day my eyes were feasting on a new diet altogether. Every now and then I'd say, "What's that say?" beckoning to a sign or billboard beside the road. I was learning a new language as well! My brain felt like it might explode.

In the afternoon we started on the return journey. With the warmth beaming in through the screen from a sun sinking swiftly towards the western horizon, I was lulled into a blissful sleep. The jet lag had finally caught up. An hour or so later I woke up to the clatter of tyres rumbling over railway lines. We'd entered the home village, we were almost back to base.

"That's one of the Blokker girls riding home," Winston pointed out.

My interest was piqued!

There was a beautiful girl with long, blonde/brown hair streaming behind her in the wind. She looked so graceful and full of ease as she pedalled casually along the bike path. My heart missed a few beats as I craned to look in the rear-view mirror to catch as long a look as possible. She was wearing a deep red overcoat, which remains etched in my mind to this day.

We had only just pulled into the yard when she pulled up beside us.

"This is Grada Blokker, Peter, my brother," Winston stated very matter-of-factly and correctly.

"Hoe oud is hij?" asked Grada.

I understood!

"How old is he?" she was asking.

I think I may have gone the colour of her coat, but Grada didn't seem to notice, as Winston answered, "Twenty-one," in Dutch.

"Bye, nice to meet you," she called as she cycled the remaining few metres to her house. I still remember how my heart was thumping in my chest! I was smitten!

· CHAPTER 21 ·

Thieves and Preachers

My sister Marg, who worked in Rome, and Winston's twin brother, James, also came to the wedding, arriving the day before. James was more outgoing and interacted more with the other guests, and I often noticed Grada and Jonath, her sister, chatting with him. A bit disconcerting for me after those initial feelings I'd had. Oh well, "Que sera sera," I said to myself.

For some reason I can't remember a lot about the wedding, maybe I was preoccupied with something else! Afterwards, James and I travelled to Spain, where we wanted to look around Barcelona. We didn't quite make it though. No one had told us that we needed visas for Spain, and we had neglected to ask. We were sent back at the border in the middle of the night. Oh well, I can say I have seen Spain! We waited until sunup, then hitched a ride to the closest French town, where we caught the train to Italy. We would visit Marg in Rome.

At the border of Italy, the train halted at the station.

"Everybody out!" shouted the conductor in broken English. We looked at each other, what was going on? We discovered the trains weren't running in Italy due to a strike. So Australia wasn't the only place plagued by strikes!

What do we do now? James and I were trying to decide how we could fill about ten hours in Nice. There were a couple of Americans in the same boat, so we went to ask them what they were going to do. They looked at us strangely and asked what country we were from. They couldn't understand the Queen's English, Australian style. We laughed and tried speaking more clearly. They were going to have a look around Nice and Monte Carlo. Good idea, we thought, but how?

Eventually we spied a bike hire shop that offered mopeds as well. We hired one each and had the time of our lives, racing all over the narrow back streets to the wide sweeping boulevards of Nice and Monte Carlo. This was where the rich and famous came by the look of the extravagant hotels, casinos, and not to mention the magnificent yachts anchored in the bay. We were glad for the Italians being on strike as we slurped on overripe persimmons, juice running down our chins. They were dropping all over the footpaths in places, the orange orbs hanging on leafless branches among those beautiful palace gardens. It was a sight to behold. Nothing like the Tasmanian Wilderness, but beautiful all the same.

We arrived in Rome in the early morning and had to wait in line at the money exchange window. I thought we would be millionaires if we changed all our dollars to Italian lire! As I waited my turn, looking green and gullible I guess, I was ambushed by a group of little kids who looked no older than six. They came begging, pushing pieces of cardboard under my nose and chin. I didn't realise what they were up to until it was too late. Even smaller children were under the cardboard, pilfering my bag, and before I knew it all my traveller's cheques were gone except for the one I had in my hand. Damn!

What could I do? They went racing off in every direction. I didn't have a hope of catching the ones with my cheques, even if I knew which one's had them. I cashed the one I had, and we sauntered off in the direction of Marg's flat, feeling rather dejected.

We had a day to fill in before Marg, a secretary with a branch of the United Nations in Rome, finished work. We enquired where an American Express office was and eventually stumbled across it well into the afternoon. I had to cancel my cheques before the gypsies cashed them in! I would be able to get new ones to replace them, but it would take five days!

It looked like we'd have to hang around Rome for longer than we had hoped. Again, we made the most of it, visited a lot of the tourist attractions, including the Vatican, Colosseum, and the Catacombs where the early Christians hid and were buried. We wouldn't have seen all that if those little kids hadn't pinched my cheques, so it all turned out better than we'd planned.

We waved Marg goodbye the morning after my cheques arrived and made our way to the station again. This time my hand never left my bag and I held a firm grip over the flap hiding my money and cheques as we travelled to Milano, where we would stay with a few of the preachers from our church who had rented a flat there. They held gospel meetings in different parts of Northern Italy, and even into Switzerland. Bernard was a chap originally from Tasmania who'd gone to Oxford University, then gave up his engineering studies to take the good news, the same as my grandfather back in 1912, but in his case to parts of Europe, not Australia.

Bernard was there with a couple of Englishmen and Pasquali, an Italian fellow with a beard. Beards were frowned upon within the church in Australia, from the world or the hippy era more likely, and were considered a bad influence. Rob, my brother, was excommunicated—mainly because he wouldn't obey and shave off his beard. In contrast, when my grandfather was preaching at age eighteen, he grew a moustache to make himself look older to carry more authority with his preaching, but now long hair and beards were a no-no. This often brought ridicule, especially at school where short back and sides belonged to the post-war era.

James and I bunked on the floor in their cramped little flat. Bernard was exuberant, wherever he went it was in a hurry. The other blokes called him the Aussie kangaroo! Bernard was in Tassie when Mike died and was at the funeral. We chatted well into the night at times. During my time in Queensland, and the time since Mike drowned, I'd felt as if God was 'calling me,' 'laying it upon my heart' to help other people. Why didn't I die too anyway? And what better way to help people was there, than opening their eyes to see God through preaching the gospel in the only true way? That's what we were led to believe, anyway.

So, after sharing how I felt with Bernard, I said I'd be happy to stay there with them in Italy. His advice was to go back to Holland and learn Dutch, maybe French, and see what happens.

· CHAPTER 22 ·

A Moment

What fate, the Universe, God, or just my own true self had in store for me was something completely different to my preaching plans. Upon our return to Holland, James continued on his own back to Sydney. Winston and Krijn were planning to go to Australia for six weeks for a belated honeymoon, and there wasn't anyone to drive the truck in his absence. So you guessed right, I stepped in and drove. Slightly different from the backroads of Queensland, but of course I could do it. After one or two more journeys with Winston to orient me, I was on my own, most of the time!

Grada offered to join me on trips I was unsure of. I remember her and a girlfriend, Janneke, joined me one day. After each stop, Grada would quickly jump into the cab first to perch up on the engine cover beside me. My heart melts thinking about it. No way was Janneke going to be allowed to sit next to me!

Three weeks into my stay in Holland, I was starting to understand a lot more, and sometimes overheard gossip which I'd later relate to Grada. She wouldn't believe me, only to find out afterwards it was true. People spoke openly in my presence, thinking I couldn't understand! What spurred me on to learn Dutch a lot faster was when I'd hear, "Blah, blah, blah, Peter..." My ears would prick up!

After six weeks I was beginning to speak Dutch. I had to really, because some parts where I went the people couldn't speak or understand English, so I was forced to articulate in Pigeon English or Double Dutch. Soon I began mastering it, much to everyone's surprise. Being a very phonetically true language made it easier. At least when I saw each symbol I knew it was only pronounced one way, unlike in English where the vowels can sound several different ways depending on the word. I was suddenly very glad of being born in an English-speaking country. English must be a pill of a language to learn as a second tongue. Grada spoke exceptionally good English, having learned it all through school and having met a lot of visitors who spoke it, before I landed on her doorstep.

That six weeks while Winston and Krijn were in Australia were a mixture of excitement and a little nightmarish to say the least. The country roads of the cane fields in Queensland were slightly different from the busy and sometimes narrow streets of Holland, where I was driving through cities and roads, on the opposite side of the road, in a country half the size of Tasmania but with the population of the whole of Australia. A bit different to the back roads of North Queensland, carting cane trolleys back and forth to the rail siding!

I would often set off in the dark, remembering to scrape the ice from the screen instead of using the usual bucket of water as I'd done in Tasmania. The roads glistening with frost could make any sudden wrong move or brake end in disaster, luckily I escaped any incidents like that. It was always a thrill to catch the first rays of sunrise glinting over the crisp whitened fields.

One day I left around midday for what was normally an eight-hour trip. My job was to collect all the old bread from bakeries across some of the northern provinces. My last pick up was in a country town, Stadskanaal (City canal), east of Assen. I closed the flaps on the trailer and jumped into the cab. Grabbing the map from the glove compartment I carefully chose what seemed to be the most direct route home. No GPS devices in those days, maps were what everyone relied on for direction. I figured I should be there by midnight! It had been a longer day than planned.

Luckily the Dutch are very well organized and proud of it. The Jews weren't so lucky due to this same fact during the second world war. I was told the Nazis had little difficulty rounding them up because they were all registered in their appropriate council areas. For my tripping around the provinces the roadways were certainly well signposted, directing travellers in their desired route.

What appeared to be the most direct path home led through a lot of country areas and bypassed a lot of the towns. My suspicions were raised slightly when the roads started to become increasingly narrow! With signs directing me from township to township dotted along my course, I trustingly drove on, piercing the darkness with squinting eyes. Genemuiden, the arrow pointed to a road just wide enough for the truck and trailer to pass.

"Oh well, this is what the map says," I muttered out loud to comfort myself. I crept along at a snail's pace, to be greeted suddenly by a considerable expanse of water - and no bridge! There was no way I could reverse the truck with the articulated trailer back along that narrow road, and there was no place to turn.

I was stuck!

The advent of mobile phones was still a long way in the future, so I was in the middle of nowhere and unable to make contact with anyone. Anyway, it was about ten o'clock, so most people would already have gone to bed that dark winter's night.

Out of the darkness, a shimmer of light appeared - and it was moving towards me!

Gradually I was able to make out a punt making its way across what now seemed a vast expanse of water! It shunted cars from one side to the other during the day. Luckily for me the skipper had seen my truck's lights. He must have been about to finish for the night and come back for me. I breathed a sigh of relief. It wouldn't be the last that night, I can tell you now!

An old-timer from the fishing village across the water I assumed, he stepped down from the punt and began sizing the truck and trailer from front to back. His dialect was impossible to understand, and his education didn't appear to have included English. Who needed to learn English when you didn't move from where you were born? So, hand signals it was.

He rubbed his fingers together like shuffling money. Oh shit! I had been in such a rush to get going I'd left my wallet in the car back in Uitgeest. I shrugged and patted my pockets, then turned them inside out and stood there with my empty hands held out—looking mighty pitiful I would say. He also shrugged and sauntered back onto his boat.

What? Was he leaving me here, I wondered anxiously? After what seemed at least fifteen minutes or more I let out another sigh as he beckoned me forward. It had taken all that time to empty water from the punt's ballast compartment to allow for the weight of my loaded truck and trailer.

I gingerly inched my way forward, slowly, slowly, until my bumper touched the railing at the front of his wonderful floating machine. Another sigh of relief as the aft gangplank closed neatly against the rear of the trailer.

Across the calm black water we sailed, to disembark into the sleeping village of Genemuiden. After promising I would return and pay, I waved a friendly goodbye to my good Samaritan. I did eventually return about four months later, but he said he couldn't remember me. Maybe he had more customers like me who ventured down the tiny lanes less travelled!

Driving away I was immediately confronted with narrow streets and right-angle corners. The houses were built right to the edge of the footpaths, so to manoeuvre my lumbering giant around the right angle bends I had to almost scrape their houses' doors on one side to avoid knocking a corner off the living room of the house opposite. It certainly was the stuff of nightmares and it taught me to never deviate from the main highways ever again!

About 2am I idled the truck as quietly as I could up the sleeping single-lane street called Assum. Home! After disconnecting the trailer to be able to reverse it into the yard using my nose end, I turned the truck into a neighbour's yard to turn and point it in the opposite direction, only to find the wheels just sat and span on the wet icy grass. I called it a day. It could wait until morning light.

Little did I know Grada was lying awake, listening from her upstairs room for my return, then watching me trudge to my car and drive off for a welcome rest.

That time seems just like yesterday. Isn't it weird how some memories could be many lifetimes ago, yet others almost as if it was in the now? Is that because we keep on remembering the memories of the memories of the memories ... I ask myself. With repetition the furrow in our nervous system becomes ever deeper. How do we remember some things and not others? Interesting question? We apparently only take in about one billionth of reality after we filter out the majority of it with our previous memories, values, beliefs and attitudes. These in turn alter our internal state and physiology, which then influences or forms our behaviours.

So all these past experiences have shaped me into who I am today, how I act, and what I think and believe. And then what will my dreams bring me? There is a saying that if we don't dream, we die, and yet all we actually have is this present moment. So often as humans we dwell—either mulling over past events or letting our imagination soar into the future. Even our nightmares are imaginary illusions in the future!

This is how a moment in the past became my future...

∞

As I knock on the back door of a house in Uitgeest, I wonder what will happen. This is where Grada lives. She is young, only seventeen and still going to school.

Her father answers the door, and in his stilted English asks, "What do you want?" (the Dutch are known for being blunt!)

"Could I speak with your daughter, Grada?" I ask...

And now, everything from thereon is also history!

• Epilogue •

I remember so clearly.

It was a long time ago, 2002. I was staring out to sea from a secluded cliff face, wondering what had I done? The relationship I most valued, with my wife, Grada, was almost in complete shambles.

Alone again!

In that moment of terror I realized the one I had truly neglected, abandoned—the most important relationship, the one I had so completely failed to cultivate. My internal world reflected perfectly what was happening on the outside—the relationship with myself that I had ignored and left unnurtured for far too long.

From that moment forward I escaped the void of loneliness.

Have you ever been asked what you would do differently if you had your time over again?

I know I wouldn't wait until I'd almost destroyed my most precious relationship with my soulmate before I did my inner work. Why hadn't I learned from my loneliness and abandonment issues in my childhood, during my teens, or when I lost Mike? Why had I kept on carrying a burden of guilt until it made me unbearable to live with at times?

I was jealous and possessive because I didn't want to feel left alone ever again, and yet it kept happening—until finally I remembered the truth of who I was. I became happy with my own company. I realized we are 'all one' and never 'alone.' Life took an upward turn for the better as I became less needy, knowing the resources within me can easily fill the void.

I learned to release old, suppressed, and even repressed emotions, and love myself for who I am, in all my perfection and imperfection.

I finally overcame my fear of being alone, and losing people dear to me, by facing it and replacing it with love. Yes, I wish I could have learned my lessons a lot sooner, so Grada and I could have enjoyed the loving relationship we now have all our married life.

Grada and I have been together over thirty-eight years. We have six beautiful children and fourteen amazing grandchildren who live within ten kilometres of our home. I remind Grada occasionally that we must have done something right to deserve this. Together we have run the Purple House Wellness Centre for nearly twenty years in Forth, a village of about 700 people in picturesque northwest Tasmania, where we see clients from all parts of Australia and some from overseas.

In January 2006 we were hit by a truck.

Literally. Grada almost died after being hit in the back by a passing potato truck as she was stepping into her car. We share with our clients everything we have learned, a lot of which was in our endeavour to get Grada's life back on track in record time, and of course all the inner work exercises we have needed to do to create the life of fulfillment we now enjoy together.

You can read Grada's memoir *You Are the Miracle, How Being Hit By a Truck Saved My Life*. This will also complete the story from where this one finishes. I wish you happy reading, and encourage you to please, don't leave it as long as I did to learn the lessons life is trying to teach you.

Always ask yourself:

"Why did this happen *for* me?" rather than, "Why is this happening *to* me?"

When you find the answer to this question, your life will be blessed, like mine.

• Acknowledgments •

I would like to thank Grada for being the amazing woman in the red coat. She was pivotal in my growth to the point where I am now happy in my own skin. Thank you for sending my somewhat unfinished manuscript to be edited without me knowing!

I am grateful to Rachel Jayne and Datta Groover for including the book writing retreat in their amazing "Awaken Your Impact Mastery" coaching program, and Tom Bird for teaching me to write from my heart.

I am indebted to Mieke (and Paul) for typing my sometimes long convoluted longhand into legible print.

And finally, thankyou Karen Collyer, my incredible intuitive editor for truly capturing my voice and inspiring me to complete my memoirs.

Thank you to all who have wittingly and unwittingly contributed in shaping my life to what I am today!

• Recommended Resources •

Purple House Wellness Centre
643 Forth Rd, Forth, Tasmania, Australia 7310
With decades of experience in the field of functional and energy medicine, we are global leaders in the transformational industry. For personal consultations, information on services and products call our team on +61 3 64283007. Visit our comprehensive website and online store at www.purplehousewellnesscentre.com.au

Subscribe to the Purple House newsletter for invaluable natural lifesaving information along with amazing testimonials of people achieving real answers to health and living their potential. https://www.purplehousenaturaltherapies.com.au/gradas-blog/

You Are The Miracle, How Being Hit By A Truck Saved My Life. By Grada Robertson https://gradarobertson.com/

www.ingramcontent.com/pod-product-compliance
Lightning Source LLC
LaVergne TN
LVHW021401080426
835508LV00020B/2401